Mildred Pierce

Wisconsin/Warner Bros. Screenplay Series

Mildred Pierce

Edited with an introduction by

Albert J. LaValley

Published for the Wisconsin Center for Film and Theater Research by
The University of Wisconsin Press

Published 1980

The University of Wisconsin Press
114 North Murray Street
Madison, Wisconsin 53715

The University of Wisconsin Press, Ltd.
1 Gower Street
London WC1E 6HA, England

First printing

Printed in the United States of America

For LC CIP information see the colophon

ISBN 0-299-08370-5 cloth; 0-299-08374-8 paper

Publication of this volume has been assisted by a grant from
The Brittingham Fund, Inc.

Contents

Foreword

In donating the Warner Film Library to the Wisconsin Center for Film and Theater Research in 1969, along with the RKO and Monogram film libraries and UA corporate records, United Artists created a truly great resource for the study of American film. Acquired by United Artists in 1957, during a period when the major studios sold off their films for use on television, the Warner library is by far the richest portion of the gift, containing eight hundred sound features, fifteen hundred short subjects, nineteen thousand still negatives, legal files, and press books, in addition to screenplays for the bulk of the Warner Brothers product from 1930 to 1950. For the purposes of this project, the company has granted the Center whatever publication rights it holds to the Warner films. In so doing, UA has provided the Center another opportunity to advance the cause of film scholarship.

Our goal in publishing these Warner Brothers screenplays is to explicate the art of screenwriting during the thirties and forties, the so-called Golden Age of Hollywood. In preparing a critical introduction and annotating the screenplay, the editor of each volume is asked to cover such topics as the development of the screenplay from its source to the final shooting script, differences between the final shooting script and the release print, production information, exploitation and critical reception of the film, its historical importance, its directorial style, and its position within the genre. He is also encouraged to go beyond these guidelines to incorporate supplemental information concerning the studio system of motion picture production.

We could set such an ambitious goal because of the richness of the script files in the Warner Film Library. For many film titles, the files might contain the property (novel, play, short story, or original story idea), research materials, variant drafts of scripts (from story outline to treatment to shooting script) post-production items such as press books and dialogue continuities, and legal records (details of the acquisition of the property, copyright registration, and contracts with actors and directors). Editors of the Wisconsin/Warner Bros. Screenplay Series receive copies of all the materials, along with prints of the films (the most authoritative ones available for reference purposes), to use in preparing the introductions and annotating the final shooting scripts.

In the process of preparing the screenplays for publication, typographical errors were corrected, punctuation and capitalization were modernized, and the format was redesigned to facilitate readability.

Unless otherwise specified, the photographs are frame enlargements taken from a 35-mm print of the film provided by United Artists.

In 1977 Warner Brothers donated the company's production records and distribution records to the University of Southern California and Princeton University, respectively. These materials are now available to researchers and complement the contents of the Warner Film Library donated to the Center by United Artists.

Tino Balio
General Editor

Introduction
A Troublesome Property to Script

Albert J. LaValley

The film Mildred Pierce has its origin in James M. Cain's novel of the same name. Published in 1941, it followed Cain's successful series of 1930s tough guy novels: *The Postman Always Rings Twice, Career in C Major, Double Indemnity*, and *Serenade*. Departing from their narrow framework, taut narratives, and first-person male protagonists, Cain offered a female protagonist, both strong and weak, as his central character. Out of the ruins of her marriage and the Depression, Mildred builds a profitable enterprise in her chain of restaurants. Yet Mildred loses all: her restaurants, her daughter, and her husband. Her business drive is founded on the forbidden wish to control the love of her daughter Veda. What Joyce Carol Oates calls "the lure of the unconscious,"[1] symbolized by Veda's extraordinary beauty and her superb musical talents, leads Mildred to destruction. Mildred becomes a great success and a figure of power who controls all the men around her, yet Veda's love remains elusive. Veda's artistic success outstrips Mildred's financial one, and finally she betrays her mother by sleeping with Mildred's second husband, Monte.[2] At the novel's end, Mildred is ruined financially and degraded emotionally. She is back in the Glen-

---

1. Joyce Carol Oates, "Man under Sentence of Death: The Novels of James M. Cain," in *Tough Guy Writers of the Thirties*, ed. David Madden (Carbondale: Southern Illinois University Press, 1968), p. 116.
2. The name is spelled Monty in the novel, Monte in the script. For the sake of consistency in the Introduction, I have adopted the spelling Monte.

dale cottage with her first husband, Bert. Together, they contemplate starting over. "In Cain, life is a bungling process and in no way educational."[3]

The book and the film are similar in broad narrative outline, except that the film adds a murder and omits Veda's success in a musical career. The film departs strikingly from its source, however, by tying into different cinematic traditions: the women's movie, *film noir*, and murder mysteries. With the addition of glamourous sets, star treatment, and a contemporary setting, all made lavish by a big budget and producer Jerry Wald's desire for the grand treatment, *Mildred Pierce* (hereafter referred to as *MP*) struck a tone and style far removed from Cain's novel. Its highly glossy look and its somewhat lurid subject matter were to become a hallmark of Warners films of the late 1940s, particularly those produced by Wald after his great success with *MP*.

Ironically, before Wald decided to make *MP*, it was most likely the milieu of the novel and its struggling working-class heroine that made it an appropriate vehicle for Warner Brothers with its strong tradition of proletarian heroes and heroines and concern for social causes dating from the early 1930s. The positive aspects of Mildred probably prompted Warners to buy the book. Tough, resilient, lower-class and lower-middle-class women who made their way up in life had been portrayed at Warners by Bette Davis, Ginger Rogers, Joan Blondell, Glenda Farrell, Ann Sheridan, and Ida Lupino. The noble, self-sacrificial side of Mildred also easily allied itself with the later 1930s and early 1940s women's movies, such Bette Davis vehicles as *Dark Victory* (1939), *The Old Maid* (1939), and *Now, Voyager* (1942).

There was also a long-standing tradition of tough crime dramas at Warners, much of it concerned with gangsters, racketeers, and tough young men raised in street settings (*Little Caesar*, 1930; *The Public Enemy*, 1931; *They Made Me a Criminal*, 1939; *Angels with Dirty Faces*, 1938; and the Wald co-scripted *They Drive by Night*, 1940, and *The Roaring Twenties*, 1939). By the 1940s this tradition had taken a turn toward a more romantic, less sociological *noir* film, often with Bogart as the charismatic

3. Oates, "Man under Sentence of Death," p. 124.

hero, doomed in *High Sierra* (1941) and *The Big Shot* (1942) but positive and victorious in *The Maltese Falcon* (1941), *Casablanca* (1943), and *The Big Sleep* (1946).[4]

To some extent the film *MP* adhered to these traditions. The great success of *Double Indemnity* (Paramount, 1944), adapted from Cain's 1937 novella, practically ensured that a crime would be added (although he had taken pains to avoid violence in *MP*). *Laura* (20th Century-Fox, 1944) was a striking example of how the women's movie could be combined with the whodunit.

Cain's name on the book and Veda's presence as a catalyst for Mildred's neurotic drives also pushed the film away from the Warners social dramas and women's movies of the thirties and toward the dark, brooding *film noir* of the forties with its stress on melodrama, the unconscious, and unsettling emotions.

MP is at once in touch with the oldest and strongest Warners traditions of the 1930s and early 1940s as it also heralds the more sour, disenchanted, and disturbing world of Warners postwar America. This division is evident both thematically and stylistically within the film itself. Its flashbacks are shot in a higher key, a brighter light than its murky *film noir* present-tense framework. Mildred as the noble sufferer aligns herself with the heroines of women's movies: Barbara Stanwyck's *Stella Dallas* (Goldwyn-UA, 1937) sacrificing herself for her daughter, Bette Davis's Charlotte Vale in *Now, Voyager* as she rises out of obscurity and oppression, and Rosalind Russell's Louise Randall in *Roughly Speaking* (Warners, 1945) as she suffers the trials of domestic life while shaping up her shiftless husband's business.

Yet these themes are much altered. Unlike Stella's daughter, Mildred's Veda is ungrateful and vicious. As a catalyst for Mildred's drive to power, Veda taints the film's central action. The aims of power become questionable. The American dream of greater success for one's children acquires a sour edge. In its path lie sexual excess, business corruption, and depersonalization. Even Mildred's nobility has overtones of masochism. While Mildred attempts to salvage basic familial values outside her oppressed housewife role, she jeopardizes those same val-

4. Released in 1946 but actually shot before *MP*.

ues by her grim drive for power and her iron determination. Domestic relations in the film are fragmented and riddled with a mixture of sexuality, business calculation, and deceit. Bert is relegated to secondary status even before he leaves the house; Monte gives Mildred money partly as a sign of sexual attraction; her marriage with him later is purely one of convenience to get Veda back; her treatment of Veda suggests the role more of lover than mother; her use of her admirer Wally involves his recurrent dismissal in a sexual role and his increased subservience as a humiliated follower who finally seeks revenge.

Finally, the *noir* framework and Crawford's glacial performance emphasize a guilt-ridden Mildred, capable of trickery and lies. As the film begins, she coldly and mysteriously lures Wally to the beach house to plant him at the scene of the murder. Throughout the film we are never certain that she is not Monte's murderer. Even when she is cleared, she is not exculpated. She made Veda what she is, and Veda, in shooting Monte, did what Mildred in her anger wanted to do. It is Mildred who brings the gun to the beach house, presumably to kill Monte for betraying her in business. While the duplicity in love and marriage that she unexpectedly discovers at the house might have more logically pushed Mildred into a crime of passion, she falls instead into the role of the tragically wronged woman. It is Veda, suddenly rejected by Monte, who does the killing Mildred came to do. She acts out her mother's revenge and assumes her guilt.

This tangle of passions and duplicitous motives and the bitter views of marriage, family, and business distinguish *MP* from such *noir* films as the classic Warners detective stories, *The Maltese Falcon* and *The Big Sleep*, in which the detective provides a moral norm that counters the often cynical world view. *MP* is also distinguished from such romantic *noir* films as *Spellbound* (1945), *Laura*, and *The Dark Mirror* (1946), in which the narratives end with an affirmation of the couple. The strong disenchantment in *MP* and the somewhat despicable quality of all the characters point the way to what Paul Schrader calls the "second phase of *film noir*."[5] It is a phase marked by bitterness, disen-

5. Paul Schrader, "Notes on *Film Noir*," in *Awake in the Dark: An Anthology of*

chantment, turbulent emotions, and the failure of love. Though *MP* shares some aspects of the first phase of *noir*—studio filming and a stress on talk over action—it nowhere conveys a mood of romantic optimism covered by a layer of cynicism that characterizes such Warners films as *Casablanca, Passage to Marseille* (1944), and *To Have and Have Not* (1944). *MP* points to *Gilda* (1946) and *Fallen Angel* (1946) and at Warners to *The Strange Love of Martha Ivers* (1946), *The Unsuspected* (1947), *Dark Passage* (1947), *Flamingo Road* (1949), *Possessed* (1947), and *The Breaking Point* (1950), most of these involving the major talents of *MP*.

James M. Cain's Work and the *Noir* Tradition

Cain's novels of the late 1930s and early 1940s constitute one of the fundamental influences on *film noir*. Three of them—*The Postman Always Rings Twice* (1934), *Double Indemnity* (1936), and *MP* (1941)—made excellent *noir* films in 1946, 1943, and 1945 respectively. Other minor novels and stories came to the screen earlier; Warners had produced and adapted *The Embezzler* in 1940 under its original title, *Money and the Woman*. But in an even stronger and more basic sense, Cain's novels acted as a shaping influence on the whole *noir* tradition. His books mirror the bleak world of shifting values and isolated individualism that was the Southern California of the 1930s and that became the movies' picture of it in the 1940s. In their urban setting, their tough guy knowingness, their mixture of strong realism and surrealistic detail and mood, their sense of universal treachery and futility, their reliance for narrative progression on the complications of passion, dream, and unconscious wishes, they antedate much of *film noir*'s themes and methods. Like *film noir*, Cain's major books chronicle the lure of the American dream and brand it a falsity.

Ironically, Cain had turned to novel writing when one of his own American dreams had fizzled. Cain had come to Hollywood as one of the bright young journalists of the early 1930s, and when his career as a screenwriter seemed about to end, at

---

American Film Criticism, 1915 to the Present, ed. David Denby (New York: Vintage, 1977), pp. 278–90.

the age of forty-two he wrote *The Postman Always Rings Twice*. It was an instant success, critically and popularly. It caused a minor scandal with its realistic treatment of sex and passion and was banned in Boston. Just as ironically, Cain's instant success as a novelist made him now much sought after as a screenwriter by the same studios that had previously fired him. Disenchantment and cynicism obviously came easily to him. Though Cain was not at Warners during the writing and filming of *MP*, he was later to become a writer there in the late forties, possibly as a result of the success of the film *MP*.

Like many young journalists and writers during the beginning of the period of sound films, Cain turned to Hollywood for its lucrative possibilities. Like many of these other New York writers, Cain held the movies in low esteem and saw himself as squandering his talents on them.

Before going west, he had enjoyed success in a variety of prestigious positions: as a professor at St. John's College in Maryland, as a reporter for the *Baltimore Sun* and the *New York World*, as a writer for *The Nation* and *The American Mercury*, and as managing editor for Harold Ross at *The New Yorker*. He was admired not only by Ross but also by H. L. Mencken and Walter Lippmann for whom he had also written.

Cain was frank about his failure as a screenwriter. "My dislike of pictures went down to my guts and that's why I couldn't write them."[6] Though his list of credits is fairly lengthy in the American Film Institute's *Who Wrote the Movie?* most of the films he cites are adaptations, upon which he did not work, of his novels. He claims he was never asked to adapt his own novels into films, though Billy Wilder says he asked him to do *Double Indemnity* and turned to Chandler because Cain was busy. At the time of *MP* the film, Cain was writing one of his few original scripts, *Gypsy Wildcat*, for Jon Hall and Maria Montez. Most of the time Cain was a rewrite man, a script doctor, not an original scriptwriter.

As a novel, *MP* clearly represented a forcefully willed new

6. Quoted in David Madden, *James M. Cain*, Twayne's United States Author's Series (New York, 1970), p. 43.

direction for Cain, a deliberate avoidance of the taut, first-person tough guy form that had made *Postman* and *Double Indemnity* so successful. In *MP* Cain sought a broader perspective on Southern California. It contained no crime; it offered a wide range of detail. It was in conscious opposition to his usual books: female protagonist versus male, third person versus first, long and episodic versus short and fast-moving narrative, history versus the present, grand social scale versus the triangle.

Since most people think of *MP* the film when the title is mentioned, it may be useful to point out the most significant ways in which the novel differs from the film, before discussing the difficulties with the novel itself—difficulties that were to translate themselves into problems with the scriptwriting of *MP*. Briefly put, in the novel (1) there is no murder, though Mildred in the penultimate chapter nearly strangles Veda when she discovers her in bed with Monte; (2) the narration is told without flashbacks in standard fashion, chronologically; (3) the period of time covered is longer, from the early Depression to 1941 rather than from 1941 to 1945; (4) the narration is third person not first, though there is much close attention to Mildred's thoughts and feelings; (5) Veda achieves a successful career as a coloratura soprano with a climactic performance in the Hollywood Bowl; (6) the setting is much more tawdry and lower class—Mildred, though she has shapely legs and some sexual attractiveness, is no Joan Crawford and by the end of the book is fat on booze; and (7) the narrative is very episodic in structure with events linked loosely, much less dramatically.[7]

Cain's plan to expand on his tough guy novels with *MP* did not fully succeed. He broadened the action and perspective but at a cost. The fast-paced action for which he was known is ab-

7. Charles Higham reports that Cain wrote Wald a series of stinging letters objecting to these changes, particularly to Wald's dramatic idea of making Veda a washout musically and putting her in a tawdry nightclub (*Warner Brothers* [New York: Scribners, 1975], pp. 184–85). Interestingly, Cain himself was the son of an opera singer, aspired to an operatic career, and made his last and most successful marriage with a coloratura soprano. Music plays a large and often learned role in many of his novels. As Oates has observed, music for Cain was a reservoir of the unconscious.

sent; instead, the book plods along with journalistic detail frequently overwhelming the plot line. Toward its end, versimilitude disappears entirely; swift changes in plot and character abound, and one climax follows rapidly upon another.

Veda's musical career undergoes the most distortion, causing havoc with the central plot of Mildred's love for her and straining the reader's credibility. It is easy to see why it had to disappear in the movie. Within a few chapters, Veda is a horrible failure in a piano audition for a maestro named Treviso and a glorious success as a coloratura soprano when he accidentally discovers her singing a tune in a parking lot. The book's resolution is particularly disturbing, offering both the satisfactions of melodramatic wish fulfillment and realistic domestic tragedy almost simultaneously. When Mildred discovers Veda in bed with Monte, she attacks and throttles her. Veda is nearly killed and loses her glorious voice. But Mildred's vindication is short lived; Veda reveals that her injury was faked to get out of an unwanted contract and to elope with Monte. At the end Mildred is back with Bert, freer and wiser, but impoverished and disillusioned.

Such wild changes clearly promote melodrama and undermine the realism of the earlier chapters, a common critical complaint made against Cain and *MP* in particular. They suggest, as Oates has noted, that the source for such actions may lie in the unconscious, in Mildred's psyche—not in the dreary realistic details the book accumulates—a theme the movie amplifies by its *film noir* style.

Cain also seems uncomfortable in this third-person voice, which he here used extensively for the first time. Oates finds this the chief flaw of the novel: "*Mildred Pierce*, . . . over-long and shapeless, must surely owe its flaws to the third-person omniscient narration, which takes us too far from the victim and allows us more freedom than we want. To be successful, such narrowly-conceived art must blot out what landscape it cannot cover; hence the blurred surrealistic backgrounds of the successful Cain novels, *Postman* . . . and *Serenade*."[8]

8. Oates, "Man under Sentence of Death," p. 112.

Introduction

The novel has a problem holding Mildred in clear perspective. Its detailed accounting of her world and close attention to her thoughts create a Mildred of determination and resilience. But when Cain takes a larger view or stresses the confused working of her unconscious wishes, Mildred becomes a victim. Often she is the stereotype of the lower-class Southern California housewife with aspirations beyond her status. Cain mocks her Spanish-style bungalow and the astrologically acquired names of her children, Veda and Moire (Ray), which she mispronounces. These moments resemble the satiric technique of Nathanael West.

At other times she is mercilessly victimized by a sexuality that she cannot control, despite all her noble ambitions and plans. Ultimately all she does must be judged in light of her wish to gain Veda's affection—in a sense, to be the Veda that she cannot be because of her background, class, appearance, and work.

From the perspective of the unconscious, Veda represents all that Mildred most desires: art, music, elegance, and sexual beauty. Veda is an intensification of Mildred's yearnings and ideals, and also of her darker unconscious impulses and energies. Mildred's money-making schemes, noble in purpose but corrupt in their original design to win Veda's love, are mirrored in Veda in a more distorted form: the ruthlessness of blackmail, marriage as a way to class and money. Further, Mildred's commitment to realize her wish exacts a repression of sexuality that takes revenge upon her. Despite her resistances, Mildred regularly falls victim to Wally's and Monte's sexual designs upon her. She prefers snuggling and cuddling with Veda to sleeping with Bert or Monte. When Veda announces her pregnancy, she is stricken with sexual jealousy. Given the projection of her sexuality onto Veda, it is not unreasonable that it is Veda who finally goes to bed with Monte. Sexual repression and the need to work, the demand to subordinate all concerns to winning Veda back, produce a Mildred who becomes tough on booze. At the end of the book Mildred is described as a plump, savage animal who flings herself at Veda in fury. Cain gives Mildred noble plans and ambitions but cynically undermines them by her constant failure to see the larger, overarching forces of society and sexuality that really direct her.

What Cain was attempting in *MP* is not always clear. He is on record as having said he tried to write a novel about a woman who uses men to gain her end, not the traditional *femme fatale* but a "victim of the Depression, a venal American housewife who didn't know she was using men, but imagined herself quite noble."[9] He stresses Mildred's neurotic, compulsive behavior as she tries to gain Veda's love and respect. In the preface to *The Butterfly* (1946), he said, "I write of the wish that comes true . . . for some reason a terrifying concept, at least to my imagination. Of course, the wish must have terror in it. I think my stories have some quality of the opening of a forbidden box, and that it is this, rather than violence, sex, or any of the things usually cited by way of explanation, that gives them the drive so often noted."[10]

Still, this broader perspective on Mildred is not entirely successful in undermining her. Cain refuses to believe that she is simply typical; she has a "squint" in her eye that argues for shrewdness of character and a tough stance against adversity. Today, with the women's movement asking readers to reconsider and reevaluate women characters in fiction, Mildred's resilience and determination may seem more striking and positive than Cain intended them to be. His own interpretation of her seems misogynistic; he sees her as the realistic version of the more romantic crime novel's *femme fatale*.

Jerry Wald's Role as Producer

As the producer of *MP*, Jerry Wald was its most important shaping force. Not only did he make all the major preproduction decisions—most importantly offering the role to Joan Crawford for her "comeback"—but he also oversaw the entire production. As the eight treatments and screenplays testify, Wald valued the screenplay as the most important component of the successful

9. Madden, *James M. Cain*, p. 61.
10. Quoted in Madden, *James M. Cain*, p. 61.

film. The many versions reveal not just the difficulty of scripting an unwieldy novel but also Wald's insistence on finding the right person to articulate on paper his conception of the film with the correct tone and the proper dramatic structure and theme. In print, Wald was modest about his role as producer. "I only block out the stories, the other fellow does the real work." [11] After the writer, Wald listed in order of importance the performers and the director. Last was "the producer who is coach on the sidelines cheering the team on and doing a general supervisory job." Yet, despite this insistence, *MP* bears many hallmarks of a strong and intransigent Wald, one who determined the basic directions and tone of the film. The difficulties behind scripting *MP* and the dizzying succession of scriptwriters point to Wald's determination to shape it his way, to go beyond domestic drama and the women's movie to a more lurid melodrama of murder and infidelity.

Yet if Wald was a strong producer and controlled his writers by forceful directives, he was also anchored in the Warners world and its studio traditions, both of genre and film production. He had no desire to break with them completely. By background Wald was a perfect part of Warners of the 1930s, an emigrant from the newspaper world to the scriptwriting department of the studio. Like Cain and many others, he moved from journalism to scriptwriting. During the 1930s and early 1940s Wald wrote sixty-five scripts, notably *The Roaring Twenties* (1939), *Torrid Zone* (1940), *They Drive by Night* (1940), and *Manpower* (1941). These propelled him into a producer's role where he became famous for World War II films: *Action in the North Atlantic* (1943), *Destination Tokyo* (1944), *Objective Burma* (1945), and *Pride of the Marines* (1945).

In *MP* Wald saw an appealing risk of moving away from war and action movies. While he had produced two Kaufman and Hart comedies (*The Man Who Came to Dinner* and *George Washington Slept Here*—both 1942) neither one achieved the success of the war films. His bent was not toward comedy. A wom-

11. Lowell E. Redelings, "The Hollywood Scene," *Hollywood Citizen News*, January 21, 1946.

en's movie with roots in realism and with some of the strong sexual elements of an original novel might prove an auspicious choice.

Wald loved risk and ambitious projects. While he regularly praised the movie code of censorship, he clearly enjoyed pushing it to its limits and making movies of subjects that were supposedly unfilmable. *MP* was the first in a long line of projects that moved between the lurid and the artsy, often combining both: *Flamingo Road, Johnny Belinda* (with its important rape scene), *Sons and Lovers* from the D. H. Lawrence novel, *Peyton Place* and its sequel from the scandalous best seller, steamy versions of Faulkner, *The Long Hot Summer,* and *The Sound and the Fury.* When he died unexpectedly at age fifty Wald was busy on a never-produced version of James Joyce's *Ulysses,* a perfect blend of high art and highly censorable material.

Just as *MP* was emerging from property to project in 1944, Paramount released *Double Indemnity* to great critical acclaim. With a screenplay by its director Billy Wilder and the noted mystery writer Raymond Chandler, *Double Indemnity* went further than previous *noir* films in depicting the meanness, venality, lust, and sordidness of its central characters. Its dark location photography, which departed from studio practice, won high acclaim for enhancing that realism. Its retrospective narration and bitter voice-over added to the mood of futility, disenchantment, and failure—especially since it was being told by a dying man.

Wald was much taken by that film and envisioned *MP* as similar—more a women's movie as its plot dictated, but one with *Double Indemnity*'s and Cain's reputation for murder and lurid sexuality. Much of *Double Indemnity* entered into the film *MP*—particularly the retrospective narration, the flashbacks and voice-over, and the murder as a climax—but Warners, as *MP* testifies, was still anchored in the studio system. Film making was more a collaborative effort at Warners than at Paramount, and the movie did not have a pioneering talent like Wilder's behind it. Wald did not see himself as either writer or director. Unlike Wilder he was not ready to upset studio traditions. Instead, he saw himself as working within them, giving them a

Introduction

new direction, combining crime and the women's movie, and pushing the treatment up to big budget glamour.

Because of Wald's conception of his role within the studio and the novel's more traditional themes and manner, its lack of a murder and crime, and the affinity of the protagonist with earlier Warners genre pictures, *MP* was more of a traditional studio movie and less of a breakthrough film than *Double Indemnity*. Wald nowhere pressed to break the carefully controlled pattern of studio filming and to follow *Double Indemnity* into its pioneering on-location realistic camera work. Instead, studio lighting and camera work in *MP* were reinforced to highlight glamour, luxury, and Crawford's star status. Yet, with its sense of bitterness and duplicity in family life, love, and business, *MP* introduced an important note of disenchantment into the world of Warners films and heralded the new trend of blending crime and the women's movie.

Wald's kind of realism in the women's movie took it out of the idealistic and yearning tradition typified by *Now, Voyager*. "In retrospect," says David Thomson, "he turned Warners from crime to the women's picture." [12] Before leaving Warners in 1952, he was to produce four more Crawford pictures: *Humoresque, Possessed, Flamingo Road* (which reunited her with Zachary Scott), and *The Damned Don't Cry*. Later at Fox he produced a fifth, *The Best of Everything*.

His was not the traditional realism of character and detail; these he tended to purge from the novel and many of the scripts. Realism for Wald meant a kind of contemporary chic, an explicitness about sex and topics forbidden by the production code, a certain decadence that allowed a glimpse of the underside of life. He insisted on updating the film and taking it out of the dreary "realistic" thirties and the Depression. He stripped away Monte's faded playboy qualities and gave him a highly charged elegance, which nevertheless concealed corruption. Mildred's added glamour also removed her from the novel's tougher lower-class and far less beautiful depiction. Though he

12. David Thomson, *A Biographical Dictionary of Film* (New York: Morrow, 1976), p. 592.

could not be as explicit as the novel about Mildred's sexual relations with Wally and Monte, he could go further than most films of the time and suggest a highly tangled web that finally seems more decadent than that in the novel, where the sexuality is often innocent and impulsive. Most importantly, it was Wald's decision to tell the story in flashback in the manner of *Double Indemnity* and to add the murder and Veda's failure as a singer to give the film dramatic impact that the episodic novel lacked. He steadfastly insisted on a movement toward a climactic murder, one that realistically oriented screenwriters, particularly the gifted Catherine Turney, found difficult to incorporate in their scripts.

Wald's newspaper background clearly put him into closer contact with the Warners crime tradition than its weepy one and he may have felt comfortable having a murder story as a framework. More likely he simply thought the combination would be potent box office, drawing different audiences. Wald's combined interests pushed Warners toward a special brand of women's movie, one with *noir*ish overtones, crime, and rather lurid sexual suggestions. The combination proved extremely difficult to attain. As usual, Wald first called for a treatment and commissioned the best screenwriters he could find. But *MP* was to prove an extremely troublesome property to script. An already overly complicated novel was now further complicated by Wald's insistence on additions and new directions.

Turney's Scripts and Maltz's Comments

Mildred's rocky road to the screen involved at least eight treatments and screenplays, several of them unfinished, beginning with Thames Williamson's treatment dated January 21, 1944, a year before the movie was filmed, to Ranald MacDougall's revised final screenplay dated December 5, 1944, but incorporating many changes up through February 24, 1945, when the movie was nearing completion. Further changes occurred between the revised final and the shooting. Like *Casablanca*, much of *MP* was being put in final script form just a day or two ahead of the camera; some of it was probably written on the set, and some was improvised by the actors and Curtiz.

The extreme difficulties of getting a workable script sprang from a basically unwieldy book that was made even more cumbersome by the superimposition of a crime story. The problem of condensing *MP* and giving it dramatic shape within standard running time and standard screenplay length was never satisfactorily resolved. Condensation brought odd juxtapositions and various inconsistencies. The movie is most opaque about the financial structure of Mildred's business. Elsewhere character motivations remain obscure, and key information is withheld.

The eight treatments and screenplays can be conveniently divided into two groups, the first clustered around two lengthy screenplays by Catherine Turney, written in the spring and summer of 1944, and the second around two equally lengthy ones by Ranald MacDougall. In both cases, excellent first versions stop about two thirds of the way through because of length. Too much of the novel—the parts where different strands trailed into episodic and often melodramatic plots—remained to be treated in too few pages. How to give some unity and direction to this cluttered material was the obstacle that both Turney and MacDougall faced.

Constituting the first group are Williamson's treatment, Turney's two screenplays, and Albert Maltz's comments with detailed ideas for making characters, themes, and plot more believable and realistic. Much of *MP* as it appears on the screen was shaped by Turney's screenplays, somewhat abetted by Williamson's and Maltz's suggestions. The direction of these screenplays is toward realism, domestic drama, even soap opera, more toward the conventional Warners formulas, less toward the bitter, stylized, and theatrical world of *film noir*. These scripts underline Mildred's lower-middle-class origins and her struggle; they support her attempts to make her own way more fully than MacDougall's, and they rarely suggest anything duplicitous. There is no indication that they were written for Crawford since the trio of Crawford-Curtiz-Carson was not announced for the film until October 1944.

Williamson's treatment needs no detailed comment since he simply followed most of the incidents of the book in elaborate detail, easy enough to do in a 28-page treatment but impossible in a 175-page script. Williamson was a writer of textbooks on economics, sociology, and American democracy in the 1920s and a regional and ethnic novelist in the 1930s. Most of his finished screenplays were conventional westerns. He did not bring any perspicacity to *MP*, but in three important suggestions he shaped the scripts that followed: he shifted the time to the present, he used a flashback technique in which Mildred talks to the police, and he rehabilitated Bert to become a fit husband for Mildred. All three probably reflect Wald's directives rather than Williamson's originality.

Turney's two screenplays are certainly as strong as Mac-Dougall's but differ in being more akin to domestic drama than *film noir*. They are delicate, carefully observed, realistic, and clear in their dramatic thrust. If MacDougall did not use their actual dialogue, he followed their general line of development. Turney's scripts follow the book closely, particularly in its clearer early parts, but it is she who determines which scenes are dramatized and which omitted, where the emphasis will fall, how the scenes should be dramatically linked, and what the overall structure should be. Most of her choices are followed in all the other scripts, even to reworking her original scenes, so it seems appropriate to call her a co-author of the screenplay, even though her name does not appear on the final credits.[13]

Had Catherine Turney received the co-credit that seems her due, *MP* would have been her first screenplay credit. A burgeoning playwright in the late 1930s, she came under contract to Warners from 1943 to 1948. After *MP*, she received credit for the writing of *My Reputation, Of Human Bondage, One More Tomorrow, A Stolen Life, The Man I Love,* and *Cry Wolf*.

Set in 1939 to the present, Turney's first screenplay moves nicely through the book's essential incidents, dramatizing them effectively with the central idea that Mildred is doing all this, wrongly but nobly, for Veda's sake. She begins, as the book

13. Kingsley Canham lists her as co-author in his filmography on Curtiz in *The Hollywood Professionals*, vol. 1 (New York: A. S. Barnes, 1973), and Whitney Stine in *Mother Goddam* (New York: Hawthorn, 1976) seems to believe she is the sole author of the screenplay (p. 193).

Introduction

does, with Mildred and Bert's quarrel and breakup, but she
underlines Mildred's flaw as well as Bert's lack of work. "I want
her [Veda] to have cake. Ray's like me—she'll eat bread and be
glad to get it, but not Veda." Bert argues, "The moment she
[Veda] was born, I might have been that picture on the wall."
He warns Mildred that "when she's got all she wants from you,
she'll walk out."

Following the book closely, she retains such minor characters
as Bert's parents and Lucy Gessler, Mildred's neighbor,
tough-minded confidante, and salty adviser. After Bert's departure, Turney shows Mildred's financial plight, her failed attempt
to win Wally honorably, her decision to take a job, her agonizing
hunt for work, and her finding the restaurant job. Later she
acquires the pie concession, meets Monte in the restaurant, and
has a key showdown with Veda when Veda discovers she is a
waitress. Mildred saves face by telling her she is "learning the
business to open her own." She presents the idea to Wally, gets
a divorce from Bert, and goes to Arrowhead with Monte. When
Ray dies from pneumonia after this trip, Mildred blames herself.
With Veda now her only child, Mildred intensifies her drive for
the restaurant with success. She begins an affair with Monte,
though largely for Veda's sake, and Veda begins an affair with
Tad Randolph (later Ted Forrester). Things now take a turn for
the worse. Mildred loans Monte money and Veda requires increasingly lavish spending. Mrs. Randolph threatens Mildred in
her interview; the marriage of Veda and Tad is "settled" in the
lawyer's office, and shortly afterward Mildred learns of Veda's
role in blackmailing the Randolphs. Mildred rips the check up
and throws Veda out of the house. Here Turney's screenplay
ends at 147 pages and with a third of the book remaining.

The conclusion is in outline form. In a variation on Mildred's
interview with Treviso in the book, Mildred realizes that she
needs to lure Veda back. Seeing Veda in the nightclub, she must
rescue her; she venally proposes marriage to Monte to get his
Pasadena house. A party is planned to announce Mildred's en-
gagement to Monte; Veda has been reconciled to Mildred. But
upstairs in a business conference Ida (a friend she met as a wait-

25

ress) and Wally, acting for Mildred's creditors, take the restaurants away from her. Downstairs she discovers Veda in Monte's arms. There is no murder. Mildred simply walks out and returns to Glendale and Bert. "One morning you wake up and suddenly realize that you're free." Mildred and Bert join hands; "there will be a good basis between them for the rest of their lives."

I have stated these incidents at length because they form the spine of the later scripts and the film. Gone is much of the extraneous and episodic material. Veda's lengthy musical career is omitted. Such melodramatic scenes as the confusingly climactic visit of Mildred to denounce Monte on a rainy New Year's Eve—and her final indignity at having to be rescued by him from her flooded car—are toned down and merged with more realistic, similar scenes that strengthen the central plot. The importance of the blackmail and check-ripping scene is built up and preceded by an original scene with the lawyers. Mildred and Bert's private sleuthing and their hiring a detective to find Tad, who is on the run, are omitted. Presumably for the censor's sake, Veda is married secretly to Tad, and Mildred keeps her virtue at Arrowhead with Monte and earlier with Wally at dinner when he tries to court her. (In the book, she yields to an overpowering sexuality, particularly with Monte, which complicates her guilt about Ray's death.)

Turney's script shows some strong structural qualities. Three major confrontations occur between Mildred and Veda: after Mildred discovers Letty in the uniform Veda knows her mother wears to the restaurant, when Mildred discovers Veda's blackmail of Tad, and when she finds her in Monte's arms. There is also good use of a device wherein Veda's face is superimposed on Mildred's at crucial, critical moments, for example, when Monte offers to do things for Veda if Mildred will be more loving. Turney's script can be described as a realistic women's movie. It lacks both the extreme cynicism of Cain's book and its strong sexual subcurrents; unlike the film, it has few stylized *noir* overtones, and the accent is not on the mixture of duplicitous sexuality and business but on Mildred's struggle. It is a good domestic drama, more humanly believable than the

26

book, but it is clearly not the movie that the more ambitious and "masculine" Wald wanted.

The problems of the script in length, structure, and tone led Wald to call in Albert Maltz for advice. Wald had worked with Maltz on *Destination Tokyo* and *Pride of the Marines*, both big hits. Maltz was also a highly successful playwright. With his friend George Sklar he had co-authored three of the 1930s' most important socially conscious left-wing plays, *Black Pit*, *Peace on Earth*, and *Merry-Go-Round*. He was asked not to write a script but to see how Turney as a novice scriptwriter could extricate herself from her difficulties and work along clearer lines. Wald may have also wanted a more trusted masculine voice to evaluate her script and to give it a tougher, more realistic tone. Maltz's sixty-two pages of comments on *MP* make the most interesting reading on the film and provide a behind-the-scenes picture of Wald's intentions and his creative force in shaping the movie. They also reveal the balancing act of bringing Turney's script into conformity with both his own social realism and Wald's more melodramatic basic theme: "A mother sacrifices a great deal for a child she loves. The child turns out to be empty of real talent and a bitch who betrays her mother."

Maltz praises both Wald's intent and Turney's first script. Turney has done "an admirable job in terms of selection, construction, and dialogue" but the script has two main flaws. It is still too episodic and biographic, appropriate for the novel but not for a movie that should be "mounting toward a payoff situation." And the Veda Turney has conceived is even more unbelievable than the one in the book. "Mildred becomes an utter idiot for not seeing through her." This problem is intensified by Turney's success with the other characters whom she has made more human than those in the book; he regards Cain's as "neurotic to the point of freakishness."

His solution is to deepen the realism of the book by centering the plot on a more believable Veda who conceals her treachery under charm and who changes subtly throughout. To this end he suggests eliminating Ray and purging both Monte and Bert of any melodramatic qualities. Maltz argues for consistency and depth of character and through these to social implications. Bert and Monte must both be "attractive failures, weak men who get onto the skids once they lose the financial cushion upon which their security and personality graces depend." And Veda's breakup should not be rendered in an unconvincing melodramatic blackmail scene, but should be based upon her "spiritual breakup when the bubble of her talent bursts." Maltz is moving in the direction of social analysis through realistic psychology. His ideas for the script look back to his plays of the 1930s rather than to Cain's novel or a modern, more stylized equivalent that needed Wald's violent payoff of blackmail, murder, and extreme action. Only a few of Maltz's ideas were heeded even in Turney's rewritten version, and when she abandoned the script, the new writers went in even more divergent directions. Intent on something more extravagant than the social realism of the New York theater that Maltz provided, Wald did not get from Maltz the kind of realism he was after.

Maltz ultimately envisioned the film as an heroic drama of one of the millions of little people, limited and flawed, but struggling and courageous. It is very much the vision of the socially conscious playwright of the thirties. Familiar with Brecht in Hollywood left-wing circles, he may also have seen Mildred as analogous to Mother Courage, another figure crippled by her background and the system she is in, but tough and unbowed. He saw it as the story "of a courageous woman—and of a modern Job. Mildred Pierce is not a glamorous woman in the obvious sense; she is by no means perfect; she has all of the limitations of her lower-middle-class upbringing and environment. In addition, she is the victim of a fatal (but typical) flaw: She is blind to her children's real nature. Yet despite the successive tragedies of her life she remains unbowed. The film is to be called *Mildred Pierce* but it might be called *Courage*."

Turney's second script manages the complexities of the last part of the novel quite nicely. She keeps Ray as a character and still lets Mildred manipulate Monte into romance and marriage for Veda's sake. (Maltz had felt that Mildred remained too attached to Bert and that her handling of Monte made her seem villainous.) As though following Maltz's suggestions, she writes a socially conscious scene in which Monte's snobbish sister sneers at Mildred and the people from the restaurant. Harkening to Wald's idea about Veda's overturned musical ambitions, she supplies the original scene of Veda's singing in a sleazy nightclub. Without much conviction, she writes the obligatory scene in which Veda kills Monte and follows it with a scene where Veda seeks help from Mildred, who now at last realizes Veda is no good. There is also a scene where Mildred contemplates suicide on a bridge, which MacDougall was later to transpose to the Santa Monica Pier and highlight as the first view of Mildred in the film. In Turney's version, the dilemma is resolved when Mildred calls the police and frees herself from Veda: "It takes a long time to kill the way I felt toward you. Not quick—like you killed Monte. But you killed it."

Turney's second script was doomed before it was started. She was caught between the melodramatic scenario Wald demanded and the more realistic treatment she and Maltz felt the story should have. And between her own psychological and domestic realism and that of Maltz with its more leftist bent, there was still another gap. However good her second script is, it looks patched to meet Wald's demands, some of Maltz's urgings, and her own interests. It is a bad fusion of the women's movie and *film noir*. It is still basically—despite the murder of Monte—a sensitive, nonviolent, domestic drama to which the murder seems appended and unintegrated. The handling of Veda's musical career, particularly the rejection by Treviso, also seems awkward, without buildup and without clear aftereffects.

Whether Turney could have solved these problems with a third script or more rewriting is a moot point. Immediately after the mercurial Wald had seen *Double Indemnity* he called her and announced, "From now on, every picture I make will be done in flashback," but she had been opposed to the flashback idea from the start.[14] Turney then argued in conference with Wald that while she could go along with Mildred's murder of Monte as "the inevitable climax of a realistic drama," *MP* was not a murder mystery like *Double Indemnity* where murder was "the *raison*

14. Letter from Turney to LaValley, March 10, 1980.

d'être for the story." "I did attempt, finally," Turney admits, "to try to develop it [the script] in flashback theme but at no time was I happy about it."

At this stage the script still had no director. Outside circumstances then forced Turney from the project; she had to honor a prior commitment to script *A Stolen Life* for Bette Davis, with the star acting as her own producer for the first time under a plan Warners had devised for its big stars to get a tax break. Davis had seen parts of *My Reputation* (released January 1946), Turney's first solo screenplay, and wanted her as a writer for *A Stolen Life*. Turney was assigned by Davis to be with the story from writing to preview. Any further participation in *MP* had to be indirect.

By this time, according to Turney, Michael Curtiz had entered the scene, liked the flashback idea, and had decided to push it further in the direction of a whodunit. Because *Mildred Pierce* seemed too dull to him, he had altered the title to *House on the Sand*. The story of Turney's tangential connection with the final scripts and more importantly her own removal from the credits of her name as co-writer is best told in her own words:

[Curtiz] wanted a lot of rewriting and Wald tried but failed to have me assigned because Bette [Davis] was adamant in refusing to release her writer. I wouldn't have been happy about it either. Ranald Mac-Dougall had been working for Wald who was high on him, and so Randy was assigned to work with Curtiz. Joan [Crawford] was most upset about the changes and the concept of Curtiz, but eventually accepted it. The new flashback sequences came through to me from the script department as I was still listed as the first credit on the script. A lot of footage seemed wasted to me and important characterization and development in the basic theme had to be cut. When the Final was delivered to me, the credits were reversed—I was second. It seemed to me a fair arrangement inasmuch as Randy had been working closely with Curtiz while I was with *Stolen Life*. But I deplored the flashback style and my then agent thought I should remove my name. I had received nothing but solo credits and my agent objected to my being second banana, so to speak. As it turned out, it was a grievous mistake on his and my part, but in all fairness, it was not Jerry Wald's decision.[15] In fact, before I asked to be removed he told me many times, "You'll be protected with the credits—you broke the back of the story," etc. Despite this, several prints had gone out with my name still on the credit list—mostly in the South, I gather, because I got some fan mail from people who apparently liked my work.[16]

The Quigley publication *Year Book* for 1946 lists Turney as one of the box office champions for that year for *MP*, hence the mention in several reference books of Turney as co-writer.

Gruen's and Faulkner's Screenplays

With the next set of scripts Wald starts the project over. Turney's script provided a base upon which his own ideas for the film and the improvisations of other writers could be added. Since a faithful rendering of all the strands of the book had proved to be impossible, the new scripts depart more strikingly from it and condense and omit still more of the major incidents. To the domestic, realistic drama is added a new tone and stance; the accent is on the lurid, the extravagant, and the outrageous. The scripts become more bitter and neurotic.

Of the five later scripts, two are by Ranald MacDougall, the final one of which is published here. His first is unfinished, for the same reasons of length as Turney's. It is preceded by Margaret Gruen's, a wildly baroque and extravagantly emotional version that departs from the book with an almost lunatic freedom, and followed by rewrites by William Faulkner and Louise Randall Pierson. Faulkner's rewrite gradually takes on enough independence to become an original script, as extravagant as Gruen's but much better written. Pierson sticks to rewriting special scenes and goes beyond MacDougall's script. She offers the major confrontation between Mildred and Veda, and she devises some scenes for the final part, notably Mildred's rejecting Monte in her office, which MacDougall later incorporated.

15. This is in answer to my suggestion that Wald may have wanted a more masculine version of the script and that there may have been some antifeminism in her release from the project.
16. Letter from Turney to LaValley.

This flurry of activity by new writers, the movement in many new directions with frequent hasty rewrites, becomes more understandable when we realize that the film was nearing production without a suitable or complete script. By October Curtiz was assigned to direct Joan Crawford and Jack Carson in the movie, and production was slated to begin on December 6, with a sixty-day production schedule. Probably because of both script and casting delays, production seems to have been held up. *Motion Picture Herald* reported that shooting on the film began during the week of December 16, 1944, and stopped during the week of March 17, 1945, about thirty days over an already lengthy schedule. (By contrast, *The Big Sleep*, which was being shot just a bit before, had only a forty-two-day schedule.) Shooting may have been held up even further because several major members of the cast were not announced until late December or early January: Zachary Scott, Ann Blyth, and Eve Arden. The numerous inserts in the script with their dates stretching from December to late February also testify that a script was not ready. And when we see the number of changes from final script to film, it is clear that even at the time of filming much of the screenplay was in a state of flux. MacDougall was not exaggerating when he claimed that he wrote the final screenplay while the movie was being filmed.[17]

By October Wald knew he had to depart significantly from both the book and Turney's scripts, but the new versions, both MacDougall's three-part, present-tense framework with flashbacks (written between the end of October and the beginning of December) and Gruen's and Faulkner's more baroque elaborations, had problems of their own. Faulkner and Gruen not only left the book far behind but offered in its stead outlandish melodramatic actions that perhaps only a Douglas Sirk could have carried off with any credibility or style. MacDougall gave Wald the requisite flashback form and made it central, but he dawdled over the present, needlessly complicating its action and atmosphere. When he turned to the flashback there was little time for the story to develop. In his initial foray he also

17. Interview in the *Los Angeles Times*, July 9, 1967.

relied less on Turney's structure and more on the incidents of the book; soon he found himself entrapped with too many actions and climaxes.

For a moment we should look at the extravagant screenplays of Gruen and Faulkner, little of which reached the screen, but which nevertheless pointed to the lurid, strange, and disturbing version that did. Gruen's screenplay initiates these freer variations on the book in a wild and outrageous way. Of all the scripts, the writing here is the weakest and the characterizations the thinnest. Mildred is a simple-minded fool and Veda an open, conniving bitch; both characters are often ludicrous.

Possibly following a directive to condense, Gruen lops off great portions of the plot: the role of Kay (or Ray, as she is called in the earlier scripts), Veda's marriage, and her subsequent blackmail plan. She replaces this key incident of Mildred's disillusionment with open thievery by Veda of Mildred's money. Gruen's Mildred is too blinded by love to admit the obvious; she blames it on Monte. ·

Gruen focuses her script on Veda's musical career, but she does not follow Wald's suggestion that it be a failure. Nor does she give it the grandiosity that it has in the novel. To Gruen's credit, she understands the fierce neuroticism behind Mildred's admiration of Veda's talent. "You think money can buy anything," Veda screams at her. "Because I have music in my soul and you're greedy for it. You're greedy for the music I can make. You think you can own it. Possess it!" But these insights are vitiated by the hopped-up, extravagant style and the almost apocalyptic wildness of the scenes. When Mildred puts Veda out, she does so with a mad fury of destruction, tossing her belongings out the window. She does not just strike Veda, but fights her savagely. When she goes to search for Veda, she presses her face to the rain-streaked window of her car to listen to Veda's beautiful voice pour out of her apartment and fill the night air. The most amusing scene is a condensation of Veda's rejection and acceptance by Treviso. After her rejection as a pianist Veda tries to fling herself out a nearby window. Mildred and Monte rush to grab her as Treviso calmly lathers his face for shaving in a nearby bathroom. Suddenly Veda breaks out in song. Treviso stops his lathering and the great coloratura soprano has been discovered.

Gruen omits the obligatory murder scene. Instead Monte and Mildred both have the last laugh. Monte uses Veda as a "punching bag" and when she returns home disillusioned and beaten, Mildred threatens her with a sentence of hard work. Veda feigns an attack; Mildred sees through it and marches her to the piano where she forces her to sing "Three Blind Mice." Gruen seems to revel in the audacity and outrageousness of her material, but it is difficult to know whether her script grew from a love of the bizarre or simply a contempt for the project itself.

MacDougall's first draft followed, but Faulkner's screenplay, which started as inserts and reworkings of MacDougall's, was written at the same time and more appropriately belongs with Gruen's in its accent on the Gothic and outlandish. Faulkner's name on a screenplay compels our interest, though usually for reasons apart from his screenwriting. His writing is better than Gruen's but his version is equally bizarre. As with Gruen, it is difficult to tell whether he is seriously executing an assignment or simply giving himself up to lurid variations on a story. Faulkner was obviously unsuited by temperament to a story like *MP*. His best writing was done on a more personal basis for Howard Hawks (*To Have and Have Not* and *The Big Sleep* from this period at Warners), and he may have regarded this assignment with glum futility. Clearly, however, he has read the book and the other screenplays and has reflected on them. He reduces much of the action and character portrayals to Mildred's elaborate voice-over and focuses instead on off-center action. He is obsessed with the contractual arrangements behind the restaurant and is rightly puzzled by how Mildred could finance it. In the book Wally simply sells Mildred the old real estate office for her restaurant. It is the Depression, real estate is dead, and he needs to claim the tax loss. But in MacDougall's version, which Faulkner follows, she gets the old, run-down house from Monte Beragon. In MacDougall, Wally fast-talks Monte into signing over the deed to Mildred even though she plans to pay much later. Monte may not be as conned as Wally thinks he is; he is moved by Mildred's desperate plea and is attracted to her. His easy lifestyle allows him to indulge in a whim.

Faulkner wants something more financially sound and believable. He makes Wally, Mildred, and Monte partners from the start. Though late changes do something similar with the film, Monte's involvement in the business comes much later and is clearly marked out as an exchange for marriage to Mildred. Wally's involvement remains cloudy, a late insert to make his takeover at the end credible. Faulkner is no help in spelling out the terms of the partnership, nor does he elucidate the takeover at the end. Even Mildred says at one point that she cannot understand a thing that is happening. With its sleazy, underhanded business dealings and with Wally chewing on a fat cigar, Mildred's world seems more akin to the Snopes of Faulkner's novels than it does to either the world of Cain or MacDougall. At times the script veers off into the Gothic. After Ray's death Veda sleepwalks in grief. There are huge rings under her eyes, but Mildred soon discovers they are the result of mascara. Quickly she suppresses her discovery. When Mildred marries Monte, Veda drinks a bit of poison, her aim being to disrupt the marriage night by claiming Monte for an attendant in her hospital room. There is even the suggestion that Veda caused Ray's death by insisting both stay in the water at Arrowhead long enough to show off her new bathing suit.

Faulkner also tries to work in Veda's singing career but he lets Veda subvert it herself. Mildred buys the critical world of Pasadena to attend Veda's recital, but Veda responds with a salacious song, a flimsy costume, and insults for the guests. Following Curtiz's symbolic retitling, Faulkner calls the film "House on the Sand," a phrase inspired by MacDougall's first draft where Mildred describes the sinking foundations of the Malibu house to Wally. The metaphor of family collapse runs through Faulkner's script.

Aside from the three-way partnership, which the film handles differently, Faulkner's only other significant contribution seems to be in casting Lottie, Mildred's maid, as a black woman. However, he did not envision Butterfly McQueen. His Lottie is more like Hattie McDaniel, a Dilsey type, who finally comforts a distraught Mildred after Ray's death by holding her and singing "Steal Away." "God damn! How's that for a scene?" Faulkner wrote in the margin.

MacDougall's Scripts and Pierson's Revisions

With MacDougall's first script, *MP* begins to resemble the film. The major innovation, a present-tense story that features a murder and puts the material of the book into flashback form, accorded with Wald's ideas from the start of the project. It gave the "masculine" and melodramatic point of view that he wanted and put the women's film in a strange new context, one of jealousy, treachery, and sexual confusion mixed with shady business dealings. Surrounding the flashbacks was a disturbing world of *film noir* conventions: police stations late at night, a frightened and suicidal woman on a fog-shrouded pier, a body in a huge and elegant beach house. This material subtly played over the flashbacks, giving them a different interpretation and lending them an element of neurosis and sexual excess. MacDougall gives us both a Mildred who can give Wally the chills with the way she makes love—a *noir* scene in the present—and a devoted matriarchal figure intent on success for herself and her family—women's movie scenes from the flashbacks. It is MacDougall who successfully solves the problem of fusing the women's movie with *film noir*.

One of the *wunderkind*, along with Norman Corwin, Arch Oboler, and Orson Welles, who came to fame in radio in the late thirties and early forties, MacDougall authored the prestigious war broadcast series *The Man behind the Gun*. His first script at Warners for Wald was a war film, *Objective Burma*, co-written with Lester Cole. When Wald ran into snags with Turney's scripts, he turned to MacDougall for a fresh perspective. MacDougall brought to his perception of the book a cold, detailed, glittering style, and he imaginatively reworked its incidents and those in Turney's screenplays. He gave depth and body to Wald's idea of a present-tense framework with a murder—so much so, in fact, that his first draft contains almost as many pages of this material as it does of Mildred's flashback.

MacDougall did not come from the socially conscious left-wing theater as many of Wald's writers did. He was from the newer medium of radio, with its emphasis on flashy effects, quick dramatic momentum, and an economical use of devices to catch and hold a listener and involve him. His appeal was ahistorical and apolitical, his focus more on myth than on naturalism and social context. Radio with its stress on attention-getting devices and its demands for clean, spare storytelling in a limited time was good training for subduing an episodic novel, now further complicated by a new story in the present tense.

With a keen dramatic sense MacDougall wisely shapes his first flashback around the possibilities of Bert's and Mildred's guilt and concludes its dovetailing back into the present at mid-movie with Bert's smashing the glass out of Monte's hand when the latter proposes a somewhat insulting toast. Within this flashback MacDougall solved a number of problems that had perplexed the other screenwriters.

He involves Monte in Mildred's business from the start, making him the owner of the white elephant, which under a special arrangement with him Mildred will transform into a restaurant. By letting Wally seemingly fast-talk Monte into this and having Monte act magnanimously or out of romantic whim, he underscores the mixture of sexuality and business that permeates Mildred's relationship with these two double-dealing, weak, and often meretricious men. MacDougall wisely sets the acquisition scene in the Santa Monica house (Malibu in the script, but a number of references in the film suggest Santa Monica) where we first witness the present-tense murder of Monte. The glamourous set is seen under several lights, ranging from the enticingly romantic aura of this scene to the passionate swimming party and the chilling death of the opening and end. Mildred's entrance into the world of business dealing is also her entrance into a distorted passion. She moves from the simply garbed homemaker who doesn't drink to the powerful, stylishly dressed *femme fatale* who drinks her liquor straight. MacDougall powerfully uses his settings and basic actions to plot the dramatic curve of the script.

The Santa Monica beach house replaces the more rustic Arrowhead setting where all previous scripts had set the beginnings of their romance. This is not so much an idyll for Mildred as Arrowhead seemed, but the entrance into a more complex, entangled world. Santa Monica brought the murder into the proximity of the Los Angeles setting and probably suggested the pier as a place for a suicide attempt that Turney had placed elsewhere. The creation of Wally's Hawaiian cafe on the pier provides an inspired link to the Mildred-Monte story and foregrounds the distorted romantic triangle and its unfulfilled sexuality. Like the beach house, the nightclub repeats itself with a difference, though it never fully escapes its tawdry overtones; later we see Veda perform her act there. Both the beach house and the pier are more urban than Arrowhead and contribute a sinister note in place of the healthy release Arrowhead had suggested. Further, the problem of Mildred's staying overnight at Arrowhead (did she sleep with Monte, as in the book, or didn't she?) had proved insuperable; here the environment added enough suggestions of sex—a closetful of bathing suits all belonging to his "sister"—and Mildred could be whisked back to her house the same night, satisfying the viewer's desire and the censor's demands. MacDougall cleverly lets the children go to Arrowhead instead; it's a more innocent place and the water is cold enough to provide an occasion for Kay's contracting pneumonia.

Especially striking in MacDougall's first draft are the homages to *Citizen Kane*. Here the detective shows Mildred photos that appear as live action later in the film. In its circular movement and structure, its beginning with a death and its fatalistic movement forward until the missing shot has been supplied at the end (here no Rosebud, but Ann Blyth firing the gun) *MP* resembles *Kane*. As in *Kane* too, images open up and are deepened. A simple murder has layers of plot beneath it. The episode in the house with Wally resonates with incompleteness that bit by bit is filled in during the film. Mildred's peculiar punishment for him makes us wonder what he could have done to her to deserve so cruel a trick.

MacDougall's troubles start with his second flashback, which works less successfully than the first. Instead of following

Turney, he succumbs to the book's elaborate plotting. With stress on Mildred's various losses the script becomes maudlin. Ending with Veda's exit from the house, his first draft ran to 163 pages. Condensation was in order.

MacDougall stopped his first draft on December 2, and *MP* was slated to begin shooting December 6. Inside this pressurized atmosphere MacDougall began to cut, condense, and rework scenes and devise the whole latter part of the script. He was aided by Louise Randall Pierson, who had been reworking his material and occasionally going ahead on her own, devising new scenes. Pierson had just adapted *Roughly Speaking*, her memoir in which a strong woman holds her family together, for a film directed by Curtiz. Her work on MacDougall's script suggests an attempt to humanize his dialogue, to give it a more domestic and realistic touch; MacDougall often had a tin ear. He incorporated little of her material in his final script but he did adopt her original scene of Mildred's dismissal of Monte in her office. This neatly condensed the complex and lingering relationship with Monte that forms a major plot thread of the latter half of the book. Using this scene, MacDougall avoided the sprawl of his earlier script. But no amount of screenwriting magic can disguise the odd conjunction in the film of Mildred's telling Wally she is in love with Monte and in the next minute telling Monte she no longer is in love with him.

It is impossible to tell how much of the finished script existed by the beginning of shooting, which seems to have been delayed until December 16. By December 5, MacDougall had reworked the first eighty-four pages—up through the children's departure to Arrowhead—mainly by cutting mercilessly, particularly in the dawdling scenes in Detective Peterson's office where in the first version much was made of his mixture of malevolence and kindness (it is still there in his insinuating tone). But even here, changes after December 5 and during shooting continued. Part Two carries no date, but large portions of it were also altered in the final script and still further during filming.

The final script goes further in condensing scenes and tying plots together by focusing more sharply on Mildred. She is made stronger than ever. Instead of stressing her sufferings, as in the first script, MacDougall foregrounds her entry into a world of business, power, and romance. By this time Mac-Dougall knew Crawford was to be the star of the film, and this knowledge clearly altered his emphasis.

The two major male roles are built up. Wally and Monte are treated more fully and continuously than in the book and other screenplays, and both are seen in business as well as romantic lights. Wally's character is closest to Cain's conception of him, but his role is amplified. Jack Carson was first announced as Crawford's co-star, not Zachary Scott. Along with Ida and Lottie, Wally also provides some of the necessary comic relief, and he extends it thematically into the more bitter role of the rejected suitor and finally into that of disillusioned sexuality. "I hate all women," he tells Ida. "Thank God you're not one." The effect of introducing Monte earlier and in a business-romantic context also deepens his impact.

MacDougall also strengthens the women's roles that help to define Mildred. Ida is built up as a confidante to Mildred, filling the role that Lucy Gessler did in the book and earlier scripts. Her caustic wit is further amplified—and still further, possibly by Eve Arden herself, on the set—adding comedy and commentary on the distorted dimensions of Mildred's relationships with Veda, Monte, and Wally. Ida has no part in cheating Mildred out of her restaurants, as she did with Wally in the book and in several scripts. She is an ideal of sorts to Mildred, one suited to a business desk, someone she can count on for help and advice in her workaday world. Yet Mildred quickly rises to supplant her. When they meet, Ida is managing Mr. Chris's restaurant (in the film, though not in the script, he is cut and it appears that she may be the owner of the restaurant), but soon she is working for Mildred. Her asexuality and matter-of-fact wit keep her from sharing Mildred's more glamourous style and sense of power. Ida is all there at first glance. If she partly functions as an ideal to Mildred, she is also a warning. There is a slight lesbian edge to her personality and her relationship with Mildred. Yet Ida has surrendered her sexuality; as she tells Mildred in scene 254, she has never been married and men treat her as the big sister type. Her freedom from men gives her the perspective to judge them cynically and correctly; she knows just what Wally and Monte are angling for. Yet this same freedom limits her power. She knows it's a man's world and she has nothing to bargain with. Her insight and intelligence don't get her power. Mildred keeps her sexual power over men and with it secures her financial empire.

Veda stands in sharp contrast to Ida, who links her with the money parasites like Monte and Wally who hover around Mildred. Like Ida, however, she functions as an ideal for Mildred. She is everything Mildred strives for. Mildred wants her love and is willing to devote all her moneymaking schemes and energy to getting it. Mildred also wants Veda's social status, glamour, and elegance. At the same time, Veda is all that Mildred represses beneath her mask of control and dignified stoicism. As we have noted before, Veda is Mildred's unconscious in both its idealized and darker aspects.

It is Veda who has the ultimate romantic moment with Monte; her passion at the bar seems far more exciting than Mildred's more innocent fireside moment after the swim. It is she who activates a sexual relation with Monte after Mildred turns her marriage with him into a business proposition. Finally it is she who shoots Monte, with the gun that Mildred took from her office to use against him for his business double-dealing. Veda is part of Mildred in more ways than Mildred knows. Mildred walks a fine line between the sexual deficiency of Ida and the sexual excess of Veda; she may protect her power thereby, but it is short lived. She projects a sense of control, a kind of mask abetted by Crawford's performance. It begins to crumble when the worlds of business and sexuality take their revenge upon her. If Mildred partly represents a new ideal for woman, a movement away from the home and into a career, much like what the war had spawned, she also represents the vulnerability of that role, its demands of control upon the sexual self and its subservience to the world of masculinity in business. Ultimately Mildred must be avenged and restored to her woman's role in the home. MacDougall's script both celebrates and condemns Mildred.

MacDougall hints that Mildred's attempt to reach her business

41

Introduction

success is out of harmony with the "correct" picture of the nuclear family—correct, that is, to a masculine writer and the times of 1944. In the first flashback Mildred hesitates over her statement about placing Veda and Kay above Bert: "Maybe that's right and maybe it's wrong." Perhaps, it is hinted, Bert may be justified in his affair with Maggie Biederhof. The result is unnatural and leads to Mildred's move away from pies and kitchens to the world of business with its harsh dealings and the elegant boudoir with its sexual excess, destruction, and death. MacDougall's script, like much of *film noir*, punishes the active, powerful, and aggressive woman with her fatalistic charms—in this case, both Mildred and Veda. The *femme fatale* side of Mildred, represented by Veda as an excess, is killed. Mildred is rehabilitated through her ordeal with the detective and her guilt. She is purged of the Veda in her, both the elegant yearnings for superior status and her more hard-edged, tough, masculine business dealings. Mother love is restored to its proper perspective within the "natural" rhythms of the family context. Bert takes Mildred back and they exit to dawn and the swell of religious music that suggests a heavenly sanctioned marriage bond.

Mildred Pierce received Academy Award nominations for best picture and best screenplay, and Crawford won for best actress. Thus established as a trusted writer, MacDougall wrote the screenplays for two more of her films, *Possessed* and *Queen Bee* (1955), directing her in the latter. From 1947 to 1950 at Warners, MacDougall wrote a number of distinguished screenplays, most of them adaptations of novels and plays—*The Unsuspected, June Bride, The Decision of Christopher Blake, The Hasty Heart, Bright Leaf,* and *The Breaking Point.* During the 1950s he wrote at both Fox and Paramount, then moved to MGM where he wrote three films, directing two of them. *The World, the Flesh, and the Devil* (1959), about a group of survivors from a nuclear holocaust, has a deserved cult reputation among sci-fi film enthusiasts. His career came to grief with one of Hollywood's greatest flops, *Cleopatra* (1962). With two famous screenwriters, Joseph L. Mankiewicz and Sidney Buchman, MacDougall took credit.

Introduction

Michael Curtiz and Anton de Grot

By 1944 Michael Curtiz was Warner's top director, having been responsible not only for several of the studio's biggest hits of the thirties but also for its two great successes of the forties, *Casablanca* and *Yankee Doodle Dandy*. Born in Budapest in 1888, Curtiz was trained in the Hungarian theater and directed silent pictures in Sweden and Germany before coming to Warners at the end of the silent period in the late twenties. During the thirties he often directed six movies a year, earning him the reputation of being a workhorse who could meet Warner's tight budgets and swift production schedules. Despite his difficulties with the English language and an autocratic manner, he had a gift with actors and an ability to translate often unfinished and sketchy scripts into a graceful *mise-en-scène* with echoes of a European expressionist style. The epitome of genre directors, he never insisted on pressing a personal vision of his own upon the films, yet each of them exemplifies a highly skilled sense of movement and smoothness. To the American genres he wedded a touch of European elegance. He pioneered in the Warners horror genre, never a big studio staple, with *Doctor X* (1932) and *Mystery of the Wax Museum* (1933), and virtually invented the Errol Flynn swashbuckler: *Captain Blood* (1935), *The Adventures of Robin Hood* (1938), and *The Charge of the Light Brigade* (1936). He had a good background in films with a hard-bitten realistic edge: *Twenty Thousand Years in Sing Sing* (1933), *Jimmy the Gent* (1934), *Black Fury* (1935), *Kid Galahad* (1937), and *Angels with Dirty Faces* (1938). *MP* united the strains of his American domestic dramas, *Four Daughters* (1938), *Daughters Courageous* (1939), and *Roughly Speaking* (1945); romantic *noir*, *Casablanca* (1943) and *Passage to Marseille* (1944); and Americana, *Yankee Doodle Dandy* (1943). *Casablanca* showed him especially able to work with an unfinished script.

Once again with *MP* his smooth and gliding camera movement covers the sharper junctures of a script still being reworked. With its dark overtones *MP* allowed Curtiz to use his expressionist techniques more fully than he usually did. Curtiz gave the present-tense framework of *MP* a *noir* style with several

43

angled and startling expressionist shots. By contrast the flashbacks are highlighted and told in a more traditional narrative manner. Within the present, *noir* lighting is employed. Mildred appears regularly with the upper right portion of her face darkened (figures 4 and 8). She seems to carry her mark of guilt with her; Bert, when under suspicion, has the same lighting. By contrast Mildred in her home setting or in the business world is always fully lighted (figures 10 and 24).

The opening sequences are particularly marked by startling shots. Monte is shown in a reaction shot receiving the bullets and falling on the floor, but Curtiz withholds the standard "action" shot that would tell us who is firing the gun; the gap creates a disruptive mood for the whole movie. Not until the end are we supplied the shot that shows Veda firing the gun. With the action completed, Curtiz repeats the dramatic shot of Monte's death. Curtiz also makes the most of ominous lighting. Wally knocks over a lamp that eerily illuminates Monte's corpse; a flickering fire strangely lights the room with the corpse; and Wally seems lost in the house as his own shadows dwarf him. Two shots show him diminished by a modern spiral staircase (figures 5 and 6). When he descends the staircase with Mildred their shadows dominate them and the camera pans to Monte's body. Curtiz makes the normally realistic police station a world of tension: voices boom and echo, a snapped-open newspaper sounds like a gunshot. Within this context Curtiz gracefully glides over the sordidness rather than calling attention to it by charged editing. MacDougall's script calls for separate entrances at the police station for Mildred, Ida, Wally, and Bert, but for each of them Curtiz elides the scenes rather than breaking them. In the film Mildred looks across the room to see Ida, who leans out to her. As Ida goes in for questioning, Bert arrives and the two exchange bitter greetings and move in opposite directions. When the reporter goes to a water cooler and the camera pans with him, Bert enters. What is broken in the script becomes in the film a smooth continuous action. One of these earlier graceful elisions is designed to fool us: a shot of the car driving away (figure 2) from the murder house dissolves to a graceful dolly onto Mildred walking on the pier (figure 3). The smooth movement of the transition deceives us into thinking that the shots give contiguous events. Actually, as we later learn, much has happened between them, just as much has also happened between many shots in the opening sequence.

Without undue stress, Curtiz often reminds us of important themes by a slight panning shot: for example, when Mildred enters the cafe with Wally in the opening sequences, the camera pans to the stage where Miriam is singing. Later we learn that Mildred here found Veda doing the same. His actors are always busy doing common actions and many of the script changes deal with these, for example, the mixing of drinks becomes a major motif for Mildred's worldliness and disillusionment. Highly stylized groupings of actors occur only infrequently: for example, Curtiz substitutes for the broken glass shot in the script a shot of Monte and Mildred surrounding Bert, a brief tableau designed to lead us back into the present tense (figure 21).

Curtiz is probably responsible for most of the comic bits the movie contains: Kay doing her Carmen Miranda number and earlier fooling around the kitchen with the food. Many of Eve Arden's lines are not in the script; the moment when she asks Wally to "leave something on me" looks as if it had been improvised on the set (figure 20). Elsewhere she may have been responsible for many of her lines, but Curtiz must have made the decision to amplify her part. Butterfly McQueen as Lottie gives a rich comic performance as Mildred's maid, animating an empty part with her high voice and much business. Curtiz must have seen that the movie could use some comic relief. Unfortunately much of the humor has racist overtones, and McQueen herself gets no screen credit.

It is with Crawford, of course, that Curtiz has singular success. At first refusing to work with her, he envisioned a washed up *grande dame* with "high-hat airs and her goddamn shoulder pads." [18] Whatever their differences, they were soon patched up. Curtiz and cameraman Ernest Haller were especially sensitive to Crawford; she is given a great number of close-ups, far more than the script calls for, and she always looks elegant, so

18. Bob Thomas, *Joan Crawford* (New York: Simon & Schuster, 1978), p. 146.

much so that the theme of her rise from lower-class origins is underplayed. She appears in a housedress only in the opening flashback sequence, and then it seems spotless (figure 9). As Molly Haskell notes, she seems peculiarly unruffled either psychologically or physically by her background or ordeal.[19] Curtiz truncates her hard-working rise in the restaurant, condensing a number of pages in the script to a brief montage. If Curtiz was autocratic to her as a director and not in the usual fatherly role she was accustomed to at MGM, he nevertheless favored her and helped her to get an Oscar. In a role that could have led to melodramatic weepiness, he encouraged dignity and restraint.

Much of the glamour of *MP* is also due to Anton de Grot, Warner's famous set designer. Originally from Poland, he too supplied a sense of European taste and expressionism to the film. Particularly gifted with fantastic sets, he had worked with Curtiz on *Mystery of the Wax Museum, Captain Blood,* and *The Private Lives of Elizabeth and Essex,* among others. To Grot we owe the interior of the beach house with its strange flickering fire, the phantasmagoric Santa Monica Pier (figure 3), the vast interior of the Pasadena mansion, and Mildred's stylish restaurants with their expansive neon lights (figure 18). The depth of Grot's sets when they are not expressionistic convey a feeling of power and vast space; they quickly became a Warners hallmark for films in this genre. Complementing Grot and Curtiz was the cameraman Ernest Haller, skilled for having worked with Bette Davis on *Dark Victory* and *Mr. Skeffington,* and, as Ted Sennett reminds us, softening her features. Here he accomplished a similar deed.[20]

Crawford and the Cast

Critics had almost universal praise for most of the cast and Curtiz's sensitive handling of them. Ann Blyth and Eve Arden were nominated for Oscars and Crawford won her only Oscar. For

19. Molly Haskell, *From Reverence to Rape* (New York: Holt, Rinehart, 1974), p. 179.
20. Ted Sennett, *Warner Brothers Presents* (New Rochelle, N.Y.: Arlington House, 1971), p. 307.

most people Crawford is Mildred Pierce. And Mildred Pierce
she would remain: the strong, powerful, stoic, determined
woman working for the noblest ends. No matter that this mutes
the picture of a lower-class Mildred or that it underplays the
more disturbing aspects of her conduct. These are there, but
they are not foregrounded by Crawford's performance. What
we see is the new image of Joan Crawford both on screen and
off, a woman who could run not only restaurants but also, later
in real life, the Pepsi-Cola company.

According to Crawford, she carefully chose this role for herself, her first major one in two years and her first role at Warners
where she had previously done only a guest appearance as herself in *Hollywood Canteen* (1944). Until Wald persuaded her to do
MP she had rejected many scripts. According to several books,
other stars had rejected the role. Usually Bette Davis is cited, but
sometimes also Barbara Stanwyck and Ann Sheridan. When I
asked Davis about this and suggested that she might have seen
one of the first versions of the script by Catherine Turney, she
replied: "I was never offered the part of Mildred Pierce. I never
saw any prior script. Miss Turney wrote many of my scripts but
this one was never intended for me." [21] I have no firm evidence
about the offers to Stanwyck and Sheridan, but one should bear
in mind that rumors and legends frequently have a habit of
turning into scholarship, particularly film scholarship.

Crawford wrote about how she came to choose the Mildred
Pierce role in *The Saturday Evening Post* of November 2, 1946. Her
statement is interesting, but, like everything else about her art
and life, it seems to be part of a carefully orchestrated and controlled image. In "The Role I Liked Best" she wrote:

The role of Mildred in *Mildred Pierce* was a delight to me because it
rescued me from what was known at Metro as the Joan Crawford formula; I had become so hidden in clothes and sets that nobody could tell
whether I had talent or not. After I left Metro, Warners offered me three
scripts, each of which I turned down. Producer Jerry Wald loyally
agreed that it would be wrong for me to take another formula picture,
and finally he suggested James Cain's novel, which I had read years

21. Letter from Bette Davis to LaValley, November 12, 1979.

before without realizing it was just what I needed. On rereading it, I was eager to accept this chance to portray a mother who has to fight against the temptation to spoil her child. As I have two adopted children, I felt I could understand Mildred and do the role justice. (p. 76)

Crawford is correct about what the movie did, but the film also redefined her image for her later career; it was a role she was to repeat with few variations. Her Oscar was a tribute to her comeback and to the sensitive underplaying of a basically all-stops-out role, but it was also, according to Bob Thomas, part of a press campaign launched by Wald and Crawford's press agent, Henry Rogers, during the actual filming as a kind of spur and tribute to her hard work.[22] Finally, the lines about "spoiling her children" have an eerie ring now that we know from Bob Thomas and Christina Crawford how well she resisted the temptation to spoil them and how she mistreated them when they refused to conform to her highly ordered plans. The following lines are even more disturbing:

Ann, as the daughter, was perfect. I loved every scene with her except where I had to slap her and she had to slap me. I have a phobia about slapping, dating back to my childhood, when my father once slapped me for telling a lie at the dinner table. After I slapped Ann I burst into tears and found myself apologizing frantically. Later, it wasn't quite so hard to have Ann slap me, but my head was shaking as the scene faded out, and then it was Ann who was remorsefully apologizing. (p. 76)

We may argue that publicity and performance differ from real life. Crawford was eager to project the image of a noble lady. Mildred in her attention to Veda seems to be almost the opposite of the mother of Christina and Christopher Crawford. Yet no one will deny that the slapping scene is one of the most powerful in the film and that it seems to tap hidden resources behind the Crawford image of control. Further, Crawford's control and determination are not far removed from what she expected of herself and her children. In her life offscreen Crawford sought to project the image she manufactured on screen. In a male-

22. Thomas, *Joan Crawford*, p. 148. For his validation of the material of Christina Crawford's memoir, *Mommie Dearest* (New York: Morrow, 1978), see pp. 167–75.

dominated industry she had carefully forged the image of a strong career woman with lower-middle-class roots, one who was resourceful and strong, but still sexually appealing, and who could hold her own in a man's world. The cost of this was the same on screen and off. The mask of control and determination shut off the surfacing of other emotions; her controlled performance in *MP* is less a brake applied to melodrama than the careful construction of a deliberate new image.

In *MP* Crawford seems to beckon and refuse her men simultaneously. Around her they become parasites and weaklings. Mildred's sensuality remains provocative yet closed. In *MP* the mask of control rarely breaks; in life we now know that it did quite frequently. Yet by this image of control and power, Crawford was one of the few female stars to stay at the top long after she could play romantic parts. Lacking the acting talents of Hepburn and Davis, she forged a different image, one of power with a strong sexual undercurrent, which she maintained into later years. In the last analysis, despite the diametrically opposed treatment of Veda and her own children, *MP* is an icon of Joan Crawford's life.

Promotion and Evaluation: Then and Now

MP premiered at the Strand theater in New York on September 24, 1945. It was a huge financial success with lines queueing up for it. Surprisingly, in its time it was not a great critical success. While it did receive some good reviews, most of these were from the trade journals; the regular press was more mixed. *Daily Variety* called it a "top class production," and praised the "sensitive direction, and consistently excellent acting." The reviewer singled Crawford out for special praise in a "role . . . which is a constant temptation to melodrama and overplaying. . . . The actress avoids both pitfalls in a smooth performance" (September 28, 1945). *Box Office* labeled it a "potential heavy grosser" and praised the "almost flawless productional assets: rich mountings, masterful direction, and superb performances" (October 6, 1945).

On the other hand, *New York Times* reviewer Thomas M. Pryor confessed to be "strangely unmoved" despite "all Miss Crawford's gallant suffering, even with the fillip of murder-mystery that was added to the novel by its screen adaptors." Then he hit on one of the major stumbling blocks to enjoying the film: "It does not seem reasonable that a level-headed person like Mildred Pierce who builds a fabulously successful chain of restaurants on practically nothing, could be so completely dominated by a selfish and grasping daughter, who spells trouble in capital letters. . . . If you can accept this rather demanding premise, then *Mildred Pierce* is just the tortured drama you've been waiting for" (September 29, 1945). Many viewers would agree. Joyce Carol Oates has tried to explain this very problem in the novel; Mildred's love for Veda is at once so unbelievable, but yet so terribly believable.[23] But to argue at this level is to accept the demands of realism set up by Albert Maltz but only partially adhered to in *MP*. In fact, the *Times* reviewer found *MP* flawed in the same words that Maltz used; Veda, Pryor says, is even less convincing than in the novel.

Most of the other critics found that the merger of women's movie and thriller was not successful and at best awkward. Howard Barnes in the *New York Herald Tribune* labeled the film "a windy melodrama" that was often accidentally "immensely funny. . . . An opening day audience was more often moved to laughter by the serious efforts of Joan Crawford and Zachary Scott than their assistants (Jack Carson and Eve Arden). *Mildred Pierce* is a laggard and somewhat ludicrous movie. . . . Miss Crawford is handsome as a matron. She is self-sacrificial beyond belief. Unfortunately she never breathes emotional intensity into a role which demanded just that" (September 29, 1945).

Time called the film "just another tear-sodden story of Mother

---

23. "There is no education, then, in moral terms at all. *Mildred Pierce* points out the all-too-human predicament in the series of confrontations and exposures of the daughter Veda's hatefulness and the constant failure of Mildred Pierce to understand. Tedious, intolerable, yes, but totally believable" (p. 124). To be fair to Oates, her interpretation of Cain is not based on realism either, but on the Freudian unconscious. "Cain's parable, which is perhaps America's parable, may be something like this: the passion that rises in us is both an inescapable part of our lives and an enemy to our lives. . . . Once unleashed it cannot be quieted" (p. 127).

Love, . . . closer to the waltz-time schmalz of Kathleen Norris than to the fox-trot brass of James M. Cain" (October 22, 1945). *Motion Picture Herald* (October 6, 1945) found the film "cluttered with unnecessary detail" and the outcome deprived of all tautness.

From a realistic perspective, even occasionally from an emotionally melodramatic one, there is truth to this criticism. But almost all the reviewers fail to look beyond these conventional categories. That *MP* is highly stylized and that it could be chilling, disturbing, dark, and troubling does not occur to them because they are frustrated on the basic levels of realism, women's melodrama, and thriller. The *Box Office* reviewer did note that the material wasn't exactly conventional and that some of the people who went to see the stars might be disappointed. He called it "far from a pleasant dose of screen entertainment. . . . The story of misguided, fanatical mother's love and matrimonial misadventures is sordid in most of its facets and the majority of the characters are thoroughly despicable" (October 6, 1945). This is, of course, precisely what makes *MP* interesting and provocative, but the reviewer obviously sees it as a liability. Only the great critic James Agee, in *The Nation*, offered a contemporary review that got at the thematic problems and the tone of the film: "Nasty, gratifying version of the Cain novel about suburban grass-widowhood and the power of the native passion for money and all that money can buy. Attempt made to sell Mildred as noble when she is merely idiotic or at best pathetic; but constant, virulent, lambent attention to money and its effects, and more authentic suggestions of sex than one hopes to see in American films" (October 13, 1945).

What made *MP* so successful was not the reviews but the drawing power of Crawford in her comeback role, coupled with a memorable promotional campaign to sell her in the role. Early trade paper ads were a good deal racier than the film. Crawford was pictured with a bare midriff (which nowhere appears in the film) leering down in typical *femme fatale* style at the small upturned faces of Jack Carson and Zachary Scott. The copy read: "Kinda Hard . . . Kinda Soft . . . Mildred Pierce . . . The kind of woman most men want . . . but shouldn't have." Once the picture was launched, however, a tease line was coined that was, according to Paul Lazarus, former vice-president of Columbia and executive vice-president of National Screen Service, the advertising arm of the industry, one of the most successful phrases ever coined to sell a picture. The new line was "Mildred Pierce—don't ever tell anyone what she did." This tantalizing line proved so original and intriguing that, according to Lazarus, it was picked up by radio comedians, entertainers, and a variety of other people in the media and, quite naturally, made the movie even more famous and successful.

Recent critics of the film are almost all highly positive. Charles Higham celebrates the film as a hallmark of "renewed maturity" harking back to 1930s realism but with more bitterness and hard pessimism.[24] Joyce Nelson's "*Mildred Pierce* Reconsidered"[25] and Pam Cook's "Duplicity in *Mildred Pierce*"[26] both offer a feminist and semiological slant following recent critical trends. Nelson focuses on the missing "reverse shot"—that of Veda firing the gun—which is withheld until the end. Cook, amplifying Nelson's discussion, sees the detective as the function of the masculine law, restoring order by letting us finally see the missing shot. For Cook, Mildred is punished by the detective for upsetting the structure of the nuclear family. She must be purged of her excess, which is Veda, and deprived of her sexual threat to the male business world. The detective restores her to Bert. Cook grounds her argument in Lacanian Freudianism and in anthropological myth, namely Bachofen. For Cook, Mildred is embarked on a valuable project: establishing the family along more matriarchal lines with a freer, more anarchic sexuality. Presumably, her situation mirrors that of the wartime period when women went to work and men, soon to return home, would feel their world threatened. While there is much truth to Cook's argument, she tends to overlook the disturbing elements in Mildred's conduct and the unworthiness of Veda. Of course,

24. Higham, *Warner Brothers*, p. 185.
25. *Film Reader* (January, 1977), pp. 65–70.
26. *Women in Film Noir*, ed. E. Ann Kaplan (London: British Film Institute, 1978), pp. 68–82. Certainly the most interesting writing on the film.

both of these could be construed as techniques by which a "masculine" writer demotes Mildred's program. Cook's view seems tenable to me only if one wishes to foreground Mildred's go-it-alone attitude as the core of the film. This is to ignore too much that is interesting and central.

The recent spate of criticism on *MP* shows, however, that the film is one of those with a submerged life and that its themes still speak to us in mysterious ways. What Agee spotted in it now looms forth with clarity, and these themes blend with complicated sexual, social, and semiological questions that lead us back to the powerful and troubling image of Mildred once more.

1. *Monte is killed in the film's first interior shot. The shot that initiates this action does not come until the end of the film.*

2. *In the following shot, a car drives away, presumably with the murderer. In the final flashback we learn that much has happened between the events in figure 1 and figure 2.*

3. *Another major gap in the story is bridged with this false but graceful elision: the dolly onto Mildred at the pier.*

4. *Mildred is luring Wally to the beach house to take the rap. The* noir *lighting on her face accents her guilt and fear.*

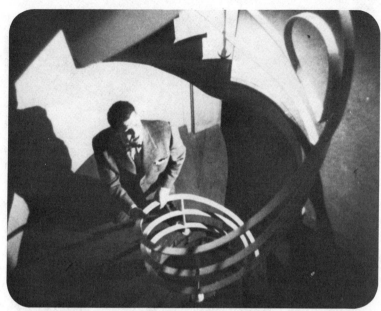

5. *An overhead shot of Wally caught in the web of the spiral staircase, one of Grot's more bizarre designs.*

6. *The second of two startling shots of the staircase, again emphasizing Wally's entrapment and confusion.*

7. *Curtiz uses expressionist techniques, here oversized shadows, to emphasize Wally's fright at being framed for murder.*

8. *Mildred in the detective's office with* noir *lighting. Here she hears that Bert is accused of the murder of Monte.*

9. By contrast Mildred is highlighted as a homemaker in earlier times. Here she quarrels with Bert.

10. This scene is not as harmonious as it looks. Bert has just left, and Mildred is contemplating what to tell the children.

11. *Once Bert has gone, Wally comes courting. Mildred tells him to leave and hands him his straw hat, a symbol of his sporting ways.*

12. *Clutching Veda in overprotectiveness, Mildred realizes what she must do to win her love as Veda subtly rejects her mother's embrace.*

13. *Ida instructs Mildred on how to be a waitress. Part of the montage sequence rewritten for the film.*

14. *Veda plays the piano and Kay dances, not exactly the way Mildred would like. Part of Curtiz's nice comic business with Kay.*

15. *An eager, almost innocent Mildred persuades Monte to give her the building for the restaurant.*

16. *The idyll at the beach house. Monte beholds Mildred in a bathing suit, which belongs to his "sister."*

17. *The price of the idyll and Mildred's excessive love for Veda is Kay's death. The family is further shattered.*

18. *Mildred's first restaurant, a transformation of Monte's white elephant and one of Grot's elegant designs.*

19. *Wally drinks while Monte begins his interest in Veda with a dance. An exhausted Mildred interrupts them.*

20. *Wally ogles Ida on his way out but thinks of Mildred's rejection. Possibly an improvised bit, it is not in the script.*

21. *Bert glares at Monte, who has insulted him. Curtiz invents the shot as a transition to the present.*

22. *Mildred as a businesswoman tells Wally that she is in love with Monte.*

23. *The slapping scene, the major confrontation of the movie.*

24. *A determined Mildred returns from Mexico. Some "man to man" talk with Ida and more drinking.*

25. *Monte toasts Mildred on their marriage. Mildred interrupts the kiss with her glass raised; it is a business deal.*

26. *The reunion with Veda. Once again Bert is displaced at the edge of the shot and in the background.*

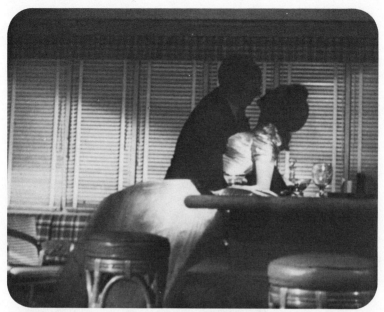

27. *What Mildred sees. Monte is kissing Veda at the bar. The noir lighting has returned.*

28. *The missing shot from the first sequence is here inserted in its proper place. Veda kills Monte. The next shot is the one we saw at the opening, figure 1.*

Mildred Pierce

Screenplay

by

RANALD MacDOUGALL

From the novel by

JAMES M. CAIN

Mildred Pierce

FADE IN

1.   EXT. BERAGON BEACH HOUSE   NIGHT
The house is lit by the headlights of a car parked in front. We hear the SOUND of the car starter. Then there is the flat report of a gun, followed by a fusillade of five shots in deliberate tempo.
The headlights of the car flick off.

2.   INT. BERAGON BEACH HOUSE
at the foot of the spiral staircase. The scene is lit from above. A man comes down the stairs, clutching at his stomach with one hand and hanging onto the railing with the other. He attempts to hold himself rigid, but slowly begins to double over as he reaches the bottom of the staircase.
He stumbles against some furniture at the entrance to the living room, then goes down.

3.   CLOSE-UP   MAN
His eyes glitter with a highlight as he lies with his cheek against the deep carpet, and one arm outstretched. He hears a SOUND off-scene, and his eyes roll in that direction.

MAN (whisper):
  Mildred . . .

The fingers of his outstretched hand clutch into the pile of the rug, and the highlight disappears from his still open eyes. He is dead.

                                          DISSOLVE TO:

71

4.   HIGH SHOT   CITY PIER AT SANTA MONICA   MOONLIGHT
                                              (WIDE ANGLE)
In the background at the breakwater are numerous
fishing boats, afloat. Others are up on jacks, pulled
ashore for the winter, underneath a large sign reading
Santa Monica Pier.

Where the pier meets the boardwalk are several cafes,
hot dog stands, and so on. Most of them are boarded
up. One or two of them are evidently open, however,
and doing a desultory trade. In the background we hear
the SOUND of a piano slowly being beaten to death by a
pianist and a singer who is also torturing "It Had to Be
You." An occasional raucous laugh completes the dingy
atmosphere.

The CAMERA MOVES IN on the entrance to the pier,
which is obscured by a gritty cloud of sand blown in by
the vagrant wind.

5.   CLOSE SHOT   DETAIL OF PIER FLOOR
which is made of planks set diagonally, and with spaces
between each plank. Dirty papers, discarded Dixie cups
are seen.

The sand leaves a light deposit of grit, virgin and
smooth, which after a moment is marked by the passing
footsteps of a woman. The CAMERA HOLDS on the woman's feet as she walks away down the pier, and then
PANS UP and watches her as she becomes FULL FIGURE in
the distance.[1]

6.   PAN SHOT   THE WOMAN
as she passes beneath the occasional lights set along the
pier, being illuminated harshly for an instant, and then
disappearing into the shadows between the lights, and
then again being illuminated as she walks down the
long pier toward the end and the ocean in the
background. As she disappears in the distance, another
figure comes into scene. It is a policeman. He stands for
an instant, looking down the pier, swings his club once,

then tucks it under his arm and starts down the pier
after her.

DISSOLVE TO:

7.   CLOSE SHOT   MILDRED PIERCE
her face whipped by the wind and stung by the particles
of sand. She is crying.

8.   FULL SHOT   MILDRED
who is gripping the iron railing of the pier, staring down
into the water fixedly. Her knuckles are white against
the blackness of the iron, and her body is rigid and still.
   She is standing half-illuminated by one of the lights
along the end of the pier.

9.   SHOT   (OVER MILDRED'S SHOULDER)
to show the sea beneath.

10.   CLOSE SHOT   WATER
It heaves and billows greyly in the moonlight. Wind
whips away the edges of each wave, forming froth in
the hollows. It looks cold and evil.

11.   SUCCESSION OF ANGLE SHOTS   MILDRED AND SEA
CUT in rhythm that gradually increases tempo with
SOUND and MUSIC. When it reaches peak,

12.   LONG SHOT   MILDRED   (SHOOTING PAST POLICEMAN)
who is standing a little way down the pier, watching
her. He reaches out and raps solidly on the iron railing
with his nightstick.

13.   MED. CLOSE   ON MILDRED
INCLUDING her hands gripped on the railing. The impact of the policeman's club down the line stings her
hands, and she reacts violently. Then she looks in his
direction, sees him, and relaxes into a dull apathy which
persists as he approaches her. The SOUND and MUSIC
subside to normalcy.

14.   FULL SHOT   MILDRED AND POLICEMAN
as he walks into scene. Mildred doesn't look at him as
he comes in close, and leans back against the rail to get a
good look at her.

POLICEMAN:
What's on your mind?

Mildred doesn't answer—just stares.

POLICEMAN (continuing; he reaches out with his nightstick and pokes down her coat collar so he can see her
face better):
You know what I think? I think maybe you had an
idea of taking a swim. That's what I think.

MILDRED (apathetically):
Leave me alone . . .

POLICEMAN:
If you was to take a swim, *I'd* have to take a swim.
Is that fair? Just because you feel like bumping
yourself off, *I* should get pneumonia? (Patiently.)
Never thought about that, did you?

Mildred turns away and shakes her head mutely.

POLICEMAN:
Okay. Think about it. Go on now—beat it. Go
home. Before we *both* jump in.

Mildred turns, gives him a long searching look, and
then, without a word, wipes the tears from her cheeks
with the heel of each hand, and then walks back down
the pier the way she came, from light to light.[2] The
policeman stands and watches her.

DISSOLVE TO:

15.   FULL SHOT   PIER ENTRANCE
as Mildred exits from the pier and turns left (away from
direction of Beragon house). The CAMERA PANS her to
Hawaiian Cafe. As she starts to pass it we hear the

SOUND of a piano slowly being played and a tired singer going through some popular song. An occasional raucous laugh rings out.

16.　LONG SHOT　WALLY FAY　(SEEN THRU WINDOW OF HAWAIIAN CAFE)

Wally Fay is a charming man.[3] He is handsome in a dissolute, athletic way, and is extremely likeable, even when making love. At the moment, Wally is at a slot machine near the window of the Hawaiian Cafe. He has a drink in one hand and is playing the machine with the other.

17.　ANGLE SHOT　MILDRED

as she passes the dingy window of the cafe. Wally looks up casually, down again and then quickly up. He recognizes Mildred. Seen through the glass, he taps on it insistently to catch Mildred's attention.

She looks at him, stops, and stands there undecidedly. Wally is making signals for her to come in, to which she pays no attention. Finally he goes to the door of the cafe and comes out.

18.　EXT. HAWAIIAN CAFE　MILDRED AND WALLY

The headlights of passing cars illuminate them briefly now and again.

WALLY (taking her by the arm):
　Hey, Mildred—what are you doing down on this pigeon perch? Slumming?

MILDRED (dazedly):
　What?

WALLY:
　You sick or something?

MILDRED (shaking her head):
　I don't think so.

Looking at her keenly, Wally sees that something is disturbing her. He takes her by the hand as one would a child.

WALLY:
> Well—long as you're feeling weak, come on in and have a drink on the house. For free!

As he leads her to the door of the Hawaiian Cafe and as the door opens and closes behind them, the tired pianist heard earlier again makes her presence known.[4] Then, as the door closes, cutting off the SOUND, the headlights of a passing car reflect from the glass into the CAMERA.

> DISSOLVE TO:

19.   CLOSE SHOT   TWO EMPTY GLASSES   ON TABLE   NIGHT
The female singer is now attacking another song. A waiter's hand enters with a tray bearing two fresh drinks. The hand sets the two fresh drinks on the sloppy table, takes up the two empty glasses, and withdraws. Wally's voice is heard OVER SCENE.

WALLY'S VOICE:
> Hope you're not sore about this afternoon. It was strictly business, see . . . It might just as easy have been you selling me out. You can't expect . . .

The SOUND of a match being struck, CAMERA PULLS BACK to a TWO SHOT. Wally lights a cigarette and stares at Mildred who is sitting motionless looking at him.

WALLY (continuing):
> What are you looking at me like that for?

MILDRED:
> You can talk yourself out of anything, can't you, Wally? You're good at that.

WALLY (shrugs):
> In my business I have to be. Only right now I'd rather talk myself *into* something . . . (he leans toward her) know what I mean, Mildred?

76

MILDRED:
Still trying . . .

WALLY:
It's a habit. I've been trying once a week since we were kids . . .

MILDRED:
Twice a week.

WALLY:
Okay, twice. Anyhow, I'm still drawing blanks . . .

Mildred has been twiddling with her drink. Suddenly she throws it down her throat. Wally watches her curiously.

WALLY:
You never used to drink it straight like that.

MILDRED (grimly):
I've learned how these last few months. I've learned a lot of things.

WALLY:
Like for instance?

MILDRED:
Like for instance that's rotten liquor. (Levelly.) There's better stuff to drink at the beach house, Wally . . .

For an instant Wally doesn't get the tacit invitation. Then he gets to his feet.

WALLY (smoothly):
I like good stuff . . . maybe this is my lucky day.

MILDRED (as she starts toward door):
Maybe . . .

The CAMERA FOLLOWS them toward the door. As the door opens, the headlights of a passing car reflect on it.
                                                    DISSOLVE TO:

20.   LONG SHOT   (SHOOTING PAST BERAGON HOUSE)   NIGHT
AUTOMOBILE
As it turns the curve in the beach road that winds past
the house, the headlights flare INTO CAMERA, complet-
ing the DISSOLVE and illuminating the house.

21.   INT. BERAGON HOUSE   FOYER
At first it is lit only by the moonlight streaming through
the naked windows. We see the shadowy forms of furniture and sense the largeness of the room and the
house.
Then the headlights of a car shine through the windows and pass around the room, coming to rest on a
blank wall.
We HEAR the SOUND of the car, which is cut off after a
second. Then the headlights flick off, followed by the
distant SOUND of a car door opening and closing, the low
murmur of voices, a key in the lock, and then the front
door opens, revealing:

22.   FULL SHOT   MILDRED AND WALLY   (SHOOTING FROM
INTERIOR)
at the doorway, outlined in moonlight.

MILDRED:
Come in.

They enter the house.

23.–24. FULL SHOT   INT. FOYER
as Mildred switches on a light by the door. They cross to
the stairway.

WALLY (who seems a little nervous):
Uh—what about your husband? He getting
broad-minded all of a sudden?

He starts up the staircase. She corrects him. They start
down.

MILDRED:
  Monte isn't here.

25.   FULL SHOT   (SHOOTING UP SPIRAL STAIRCASE)

MILDRED (continuing):
  Besides—you can talk your way out of anything . . .

WALLY (shrugs):
  I get by. (Puzzled.) But you keep saying that.

MILDRED:
  Do I?

They reach the door of the den and enter.[5]

MILDRED:
  Will you make a drink or shall I?

WALLY:
  Let me see if I remember how.

26.   FULL SHOT   INT. BAR AND DEN
as Mildred and Wally enter. She switches on the lights,
which also illuminate the back bar. Opposite the bar is
the entrance to another room.
  Wally goes to the bar and starts mixing two drinks.
Occasionally he looks at Mildred with a puzzled air.

MILDRED:
  You don't seem very happy to be here, Wally.

WALLY (from the bar):
  Oh, I'm happy enough. Believe me—inside my
  heart is singing.

He grins at her as he crosses with the drinks.

MILDRED (shaking her head):
  Pretty corny, Wally.

WALLY (sitting down in opposite easy chair):
  I'm a corny guy. But smart. I wonder about things.

For instance— (he looks at her levelly) I wonder why you brought me here. All of a sudden, voom! Husband away. Quiet room. Soft lights. (He pauses.) Opportunity. Why?

MILDRED (poking at the ice in her glass with a forefinger):
Maybe I find you irresistible.

WALLY (he looks at her carefully):
You make me shiver, Mildred. You always have.

MILDRED (murmuring):
You make love so nicely, Wally. (Mimicking his tone.) You always have.

WALLY:
All my life when I've wanted something, I've gone after it, Mildred . . . and I get it. Maybe it takes me a little time here and there. Okay, but I get what I want.

MILDRED:
That must be nice.

WALLY:
Yeah. It is.

She looks at him calmly, and he at her. Then he slowly and confidently leans forward and kisses her mouth.[6] She deliberately knocks the drink off the coffee table to the floor. They break apart as Mildred looks at the floor. Wally glances at her narrowly.

WALLY:
What's the score?

MILDRED (softly):
I feel a little sticky. Maybe I'd better change my dress. (She smiles.)

WALLY (mollified and grinning widely):
Yeah. Sure, Mildred. That's a good idea.

MILDRED (going toward the other room):
   I'll only be a minute.

WALLY (going to the bar):
   Leave the door open . . . (He looks at her in the mirror.) We can talk.

Mildred goes into the bedroom.

MILDRED'S VOICE (from the bedroom; OVER SCENE and muffled):
   All right. I like to hear you talk.

WALLY (grinning):
   So do I. There's something about the sound of my own voice that fascinates me.[7] (He drinks heavily.) Anyhow, I'm glad you're not sore at me, Mildred. I can't help myself. With me being smart is a disease. Know what I mean?

27.   CLOSE   ON BEDROOM DOOR
   as it closes softly. The latch clicks.

28.   CLOSE   ON WALLY
   He looks up expectantly.

WALLY (picking up the two drinks):
   Hey—say something. This one-way conversation is boring me. (He crosses to the door.) Hey—your drink is getting cold.

There is no answer. Looking puzzled and a little annoyed, Wally tries the door. It is locked. Wally sets the drinks down.

WALLY:
   Listen, Mildred . . . don't play games. I'm a nice guy up to a certain point.[8]

No answer. Wally begins pounding on the door.

29.   INT. BEDROOM
   The lights are out. One of the windows is open, the

curtains blowing into the room. Framed in the window, as CAMERA MOVES IN to it, we see a distant figure running along the beach.

WALLY'S VOICE (OVER SCENE):
Hey—what's the matter with you?

30.   FULL SHOT   FOYER
as Wally comes tearing out of the den and up the stairs. He bumps into some of the furniture on the way, which doesn't improve his disposition.

31.   SERIES OF SHOTS
Wally searching the rooms of the house for Mildred. The only light is moonlight and the occasional headlights of passing cars which flicker briefly around the walls. He keeps up a steady monologue of muttered vituperation.

WALLY:
What kind of a business *is* this . . . Nobody gives *me* the needle. Nobody! Mildred! Mildred![9]

32.   FULL SHOT   LIVING ROOM ENTRANCE
as Wally passes. He trips over the cord of the lamp in the recess, causing it to fall. For the first time its rays shine into the living room along the floor. With a muffled exclamation Wally leans down to pick it up. Then he freezes cold, looking at something.

33.–34. OMITTED

35.   FULL SHOT   WALLY AND BODY
the dead body of Monte Beragon is outlined by the lamplight. Wally is petrified.

WALLY:
Monte?

He goes to the body, then sees a gun lying on the floor. He backs away slowly, whistling soundlessly.

36. CLOSE ON WALLY
    He is perspiring heavily and his face twitches nervously
    as he looks desperately around the room, wondering
    what to do. He starts toward the telephone.

37. CLOSE ON PHONE
    with Wally's hand coming INTO SCENE, reaching for it.
    Suddenly it rings harshly!

38. CLOSE ON WALLY
    as he jerks his hand away from the vicinity of phone and
    starts backing away. The SOUND of phone continues
    OVER SCENE.

39. OMITTED

40.–41. ANOTHER ANGLE WALLY
    as he tries the front door. It won't open. It's locked. He
    looks around desperately. For an instant he is in
    silhouette as the headlights of a car shine through the
    graceful bay window off the foyer. Then he kicks out the
    window frame and then starts climbing through.

42. INT. SQUAD CAR SHOT
    which contains two burly policemen. The headlights of
    their cars are those that illuminated Wally as he went
    through the window. One of the policemen is tense.

    MARKEY:
        Hey—you see that?

    Jones, the policeman driving, slams on the brakes. The
    car squeals to a stop, slowing around.

    JONES:
        See what?

    MARKEY:
        Hit that house with the light. I thought I saw—

Jones obediently switches on his searchlight and flicks it against the house. We see the running figure of Wally. Markey is halfway out of the car.

MARKEY:
> There he is! (Shouting.) Stop, you! (Then to Jones.) Run him down!

43. FOLLOW SHOT   ON WALLY
SHOOTING past Markey, who is on the running board. The squad car chases over the sand after Wally, who is lit up in the glaring spotlight.

44. SIDE ANGLE SHOT   MARKEY
as he unholsters an automatic and fires.

45. FOLLOW SHOT   ON WALLY
a fountain of sand is kicked up ahead of him by the bullet. He stops immediately, shaking and trembling, and turns to face the policeman.

46. FULL SHOT   WALLY
In the background we hear the SOUND of the car doors slamming, and then the two policemen come into scene. Jones's hands travel over Wally in a quick frisk.

JONES:
> No gun.

MARKEY (to Wally):
> What's your hurry, pal? (To Jones.) Better take a look in the house and see what's going on. This guy came through that front window like he was shot out of a cannon.

Jones grunts and starts away out of scene. Markey half helps, half pushes Wally down the beam of light toward the car. Wally's arm is bleeding.

WALLY (bitterly):
　　I'm so smart it's a disease. Oh, brother.

Wally sits on the running board of the car. Markey turns
the searchlight so it shines on Wally, then sees the cut
on his arm.

MARKEY:
　　Got that going through the window, huh?

WALLY:
　　Naw—I cut myself shaving.

Markey reaches into the car for a first aid kit.

46A.　　TWO SHOT　WALLY AND MARKEY
　　as the policeman prepares a bandage. He looks Wally
　　over carefully.

　　MARKEY:
　　　What were you doing in that house, pal? Picking up
　　　some souvenirs, maybe?

　　WALLY (sour):
　　　No, pal. Nothing petty. This is a big night in your
　　　life. Lots of excitement. (He pauses.) There's a stiff
　　　in there.

　　MARKEY (freezes for a second):
　　　And I suppose you were just running down to the
　　　station to report it, huh? (Jones enters; to Jones.) He
　　　says there's a dead guy in the house.

　　JONES (calmly):
　　　You never saw a deader.

　　Markey and Jones look at Wally solemnly for an instant.
　　Then Markey starts around to the other side of the car.

47.　　CLOSE　ON MARKEY
　　as he opens car door on the right and reaches in to pick
　　up his radio microphone. He switches it on.

MARKEY:
> Car 93 to KQVB . . . 93 calling KQVB . . .

DISSOLVE TO:

48.   PAN SHOT   PASSENGER BUS   NIGHT
marked Pasadena.[10] It comes in and stops at a corner opposite the CAMERA, then goes on out-of-scene, revealing Mildred, who has just got off. She starts across street TOWARD CAMERA.

49.   CLOSE SHOT   DOOR TO MANSION
Mildred's shadow falls across the door. CAMERA DOLLIES CLOSE on her hands as she fits the key in the door.

50.   INT. PASADENA HOUSE (FOYER SIDE ANGLE)
as Mildred enters wearily. She is just taking off her gloves as Veda comes running into scene.

Veda Pierce is eighteen or nineteen years old at this point. Her poise is such, however, that she seems older. Normally she is a remarkably self-confident girl, very much interested in herself. At the moment, however, Veda is not poised. She is very much upset, as she clutches at her mother.

VEDA:
> Mother! Where have you been? What's happened? They won't tell me anything.

MILDRED:
> Who won't tell you anything? Who is "they"?

Without turning Veda nods her head, over her shoulder. Mildred looks up and her face is suddenly gaunt.

51.   ANOTHER ANGLE (OVER MILDRED'S SHOULDER)
Standing in the doorway of the living room beyond are two detectives. Both wear topcoats and are carrying their hats in their hands. The taller of the two is evidently the boss. He does all the talking.

DETECTIVE:
  Mrs. Beragon? We're from headquarters.

52.   CLOSE   ON MILDRED   (WITH VEDA)
as they look at each other, then back to detectives.

DETECTIVE'S VOICE (OVER SCENE):
  The inspector would like you to come down and
  talk a little with him . . . if it's convenient.

VEDA (turning to face detectives):
  Why? What's the matter?

53.   CLOSE   ON DETECTIVES

DETECTIVE (awkwardly):
  Sorry, young lady. We only *ask* questions. Besides
  (he looks at his partner, who shifts uneasily from
  foot to foot) we don't rightly know what the trouble is. (Soothingly.) Probably just something about
  the car—or something.

54.   TWO SHOT   MILDRED AND VEDA
Veda is almost shielding her mother.

VEDA (savagely):
  At this time of night?

Mildred turns Veda around to face her.

MILDRED:
  It's all right, dear. Whatever it is, I'll take care of it.
  And don't think about it. Please. Go to bed.

Reluctantly Veda relaxes and starts toward the stairway,
looking back at her mother.

55.   FULL SHOT   (FOYER)
Mildred turns to the detectives. The three of them start
toward the door.

56. DOLLY SHOT   GROUP

DETECTIVE (he looks up the stairs):
I couldn't say nothing in front of the girl . . .

MILDRED (in a low voice):
What's the matter?

DETECTIVE (twisting his hat):
Mr. Beragon—your husband—he's been murdered.

Silently, with no expression, and on leaden feet, Mildred turns and walks toward the front door, the detectives following.[11]

DISSOLVE TO:

57. CLOSE SHOT   (WIDE ANGLE)   NIGHT
of the sign cut into the stone over the doorway of the Los Angeles Police Department. The CAMERA PANS DOWN to reveal Mildred Pierce, flanked by the two detectives, just entering the building.

DISSOLVE TO:

58. TRAVELING SHOT   LONG CORRIDOR
as the three walk along. On one side are tall windows, through which we catch an occasional glimpse of the night sky outside.

In the center of the corridor opposite the windows is a bank of elevators. A scrubwoman is cleaning the marble floors.

Also opposite the windows, on either side of the elevators, are rows of offices with glass-paneled doors and various corridors leading off the main hall.

The three people stop at one of the doors.

59. FULL FRONT SHOT   MILDRED AND OTHERS
The room is numbered 209 on the stippled glass. On the wall beside the door is painted in gold and black letters Criminal Investigations Division. Under the sign is a stylized hand pointing a peremptory finger at the doorknob. Mildred goes in the open door, followed by the tall detective.[12]

60.   INT. ANTEROOM   CRIMINAL INVESTIGATIONS DIVISION
This is a small cubbyhole of a reception office, with one
or two hard-backed chairs. The anteroom is formed by
stippled glass-paned partitions. There is a door at the
right as you enter, and a bank teller type wicket on the
left.
A man wearing a hat appears at the wicket in answer
to a knock by the detective.

ED (the man with the hat):
Hiya, Joe. What you got?

JOE (indicating Mildred):
This is Mrs. Pierce . . . I mean Beragon.

ED:
Which is it . . . Pierce or Beragon . . . Make up yer
mind.

MILDRED:
Mildred Pierce Beragon.

ED:
Okay. Wheel her in.

There is the SOUND of a door buzzer, and the detective
opens the door of the anteroom and gestures Mildred
in. She enters.

61.   FULL SHOT   INT. LARGE ROOM
as Mildred enters. Ed, the detective, motions her to a
seat underneath a clock on the wall.

ED:
Sit over there. (Into interoffice phone.) Mrs. Beragon just came in.

INTEROFFICE VOICE:
Tell her we'll be right with her.

ED (to Mildred):
Guess you heard that. (She nods.)

The door at the end of the room opens, and Ida comes in, escorted by a matron. Mildred rises in reaction . . .

ED (to matron):
    Go right in.

MILDRED:
    Ida . . . (Ida reacts.)

ED:
    No talking . . .

Ida goes toward Peterson's office, looking back at Mildred worriedly. Peterson's door opens, and Wally comes out, escorted by Markey, the policeman.

ED (as Wally goes by):
    We'll dust off your old room . . . the one with the view.

WALLY (grimly):
    Hah-hah. Big joke. (He sees Mildred and stops.) You—

MILDRED:
    Wally, I—

ED:
    No talking . . .

Wally is taken to the door marked Fingerprint Section and goes out. Mildred sits down slowly. The CAMERA PANS UP to the clock, which ticks loudly. The time is 1:35.[13]

DISSOLVE TO:

62. CLOSE ON CLOCK
    which now reads 1:55. The CAMERA PANS DOWN to Mildred, who is getting more and more nervous. We hear the SOUND of the clock, and the monotonous squeaking of Ed's chair as he rocks back and forth, in the background. He's occupied in trying to roll a cigarette.

The door of the anteroom opens and a reporter comes wandering in.

REPORTER:
  What's the good word?

ED (who never looks at him):
  My feet hurt, that's the good word.

REPORTER:
  You got me crying. How about a nice juicy item for the morning edition? (He's poking into things on Ed's desk, looking at Mildred.) What's she in for?

ED (still working on his cigarette):
  Parking gum under her seat in the movies. Scram.

The reporter wanders out the way he came. Ed finally gives up on the cigarette and throws it away, settling for a snipe from the ashtray. The door in back opens, and Bert Pierce comes in, under escort.

63. MED. CLOSE   ON MILDRED
  as she reacts to Bert's entrance. This shakes her greatly, more than the others.

MILDRED:
  Bert—

Bert and the detective pass between Mildred and the CAMERA.

DETECTIVE (to Mildred):
  No talking . . .

Bert and the detective go on to Peterson's office.[14]

64. ANOTHER ANGLE   MILDRED AND ED

ED (to Mildred):
  You know that guy?

MILDRED (tonelessly):
> Yes. We were married once.

We hear the SOUND of the clock, and then again the monotonous squeaking of Ed's chair.

DISSOLVE TO:

65.–75. CLOSE ON CLOCK (BOOM SHOT)
which now reads 2:25. The CAMERA BOOMS DOWN and BACK for a FULL SHOT of the room, which seems like a funnel leading to Peterson's door.
Ed is still rocking. Mildred is still sitting.
Then suddenly with a harsh abruptness that makes Mildred jump, a buzzer SOUNDS.
Ed looks at Mildred.

ED:
> They want *you* now. (Mildred gets up and starts for door slowly.) Now you can talk.

Mildred goes to Peterson's door, squares her shoulders, then enters. The door closes behind her.[15]

76. FULL SHOT INT. INSPECTOR'S OFFICE
which is fairly large and rather cold looking. The desk beneath the high windows is cluttered with souvenirs.

PETERSON:
> Won't you sit down, Mrs. Beragon . . . (Indicating chair close to desk.)

Mildred sits down. Peterson sits on a corner of his desk and continues pleasantly, his manner half-embarrassed.

PETERSON:
> Uh—sorry about your husband. It must be a shock to you. (Mildred nods; he laughs apologetically.) I'm afraid I don't quite know how to begin. The fact of the matter is, Mrs. Beragon, that— (he gets up and walks around his desk) we don't need you. (He sits down in his chair.)

Mildred is totally unprepared for this and doesn't quite understand.

MILDRED:
You don't need me?

PETERSON (gesturing helplessly):
I don't know how to apologize for bringing you down here for nothing . . . but you understand— we had to be sure.

77.   CLOSE-UP PETERSON
He is half-smiling pleasantly, but his eyes are cold and calculating as he looks at Mildred.

PETERSON:
Now we're sure.

78.   CLOSE ON MILDRED

MILDRED (tonelessly):
You're not going to ask me questions? I thought you'd ask me questions.

79.   TWO SHOT FAVORING PETERSON
as he gets up from his desk chair and comes around in front again.

PETERSON:
I know, Mrs. Beragon. Everybody thinks detectives do nothing but ask questions—but, detectives got a soul same as anybody. Cigarette? (He extends a case from the desk. Mildred shakes her head.) Go ahead. Won't hurt you. (She takes one.) Why heck, Mrs. Beragon— (he lights his cigarette) being a detective is like—like making an automobile. You just take all the pieces and put 'em together one by one, and first thing you know you got an automobile— (he pauses) or a murderer.

He goes around his desk again and sits down.

PETERSON:
And we got him. You're in the clear, Mrs. Beragon.
The case is on ice. You can go now.

Mildred gets to her feet. She is indecisive for an instant.
Then,

MILDRED:
Could you—would you tell me who—who—

PETERSON:
Who did it? Sure. You're entitled to know.

He rings a buzzer.

80.–83. OMITTED

84.   FULL SHOT   PETERSON'S OFFICE
as Peterson leans back in his chair, watching Mildred for
her reaction. Mildred stands, looking at the door. Bert
Pierce comes in, followed by a detective.

PETERSON:
He did it, Mrs. Beragon. Your first husband.

MILDRED:
Not Bert—no! (To Peterson, desperately.) He didn't
do it.

PETERSON:
Ask him.

Mildred faces Bert. He looks at her, saying nothing.
Then his eyes drop.

PETERSON (to Mildred, cheerfully):
He did it all right.

MILDRED (to Bert):
No, Bert! I won't let you do this! (To Peterson, savagely.) What about Wally Fay? How do you know
he didn't do it?

PETERSON:
Fay had no motive. This guy— (indicating Bert) did.
You see, Mrs. Beragon, we start out with nothing.
Just a corpse . . . if you'll pardon the expression.
Okay. We look at the corpse . . . and we say why?
What was the reason? And when we find the rea-
son, we find the guy that made the corpse. (Point-
ing with his thumb.) In this case—him.

Peterson makes a motion of dismissal. Bert is taken out
with a last long look at Mildred. She turns to the inspector.

MILDRED (desperately):
I tell you Bert didn't do it! I *know* he didn't.

PETERSON:
Do you? (Produces a gun from his drawer.) The
murder was committed with this. Know who it belongs to?

MILDRED:
I—I don't know.

PETERSON:
We do. It belongs to Pierce. That's fact number one.
Fact number two . . . he doesn't deny killing Beragon. He seemed to think it was a good idea. (He
leans back.) And if there's one thing we know from
experience, Mrs. Beragon, it's that an innocent man
always denies the crime . . . loud and often. (He
shrugs.) Pierce doesn't. Do you blame us for feeling
fairly confident that he's the guy that put four shots
out of six into Beragon?

MILDRED:
He didn't. He couldn't. He's too kind . . . and gentle . . .

PETERSON:
Okay. He's kind and gentle. He's wonderful. (A

pause.) If he's so wonderful, Mrs. Beragon . . .
why did you divorce him?

MILDRED:
I was wrong. It's taken me four years to find that
out. Now I know— I was wrong.

PETERSON (leaning back):
Let's see . . . four years ago, Bert was in the real
estate business, wasn't he?

MILDRED:
Yes . . . He and Wally Fay were partners. For a
long time they made good money. They built a lot
of houses. Then suddenly people stopped buying.
The boom was over.

DISSOLVE TO:

85.–87. FULL SHOT   EXT. REAL ESTATE OFFICE
Bert is outside as the mailman approaches.

MILDRED'S VOICE (OVER SCENE):
And then one day Bert and Wally split up. Wally
was in. Bert was out. But I didn't know that. Bert
didn't tell me when he came home that day.

BERT (to mailman):
Got a change of address card?

MAILMAN:
Sure.[16]

DISSOLVE TO:

88.   PAN SHOT   BERT
approaching the Pierce home.

MILDRED'S VOICE:
This is where we lived. 114 Corvalis Street . . .

89.   INT. PIERCE HOME   KITCHEN
Mildred is putting the icing on a magnificent birthday
cake. This is a vastly different Mildred from the one we

are now accustomed to. At this point she looks harried and not too well kept.

MILDRED'S VOICE (continuing OVER):
> I was always in the kitchen. I felt as though I'd been born in a kitchen and lived there all my life, except for the few hours it took to get married.[17]

Bert comes in the kitchen door. The screen door slams behind him.

MILDRED (not looking):
> That you, Bert?

BERT (sullenly):
> Yeah. Who else?

MILDRED (looking up; pleasantly):
> I thought it might be Mrs. Whitley calling for her cake. (She indicates.)

BERT (irritated):
> Well, it isn't.

Bert goes on through the kitchen.

90.   INT. LIVING ROOM
The CAMERA HOLDS on an upright piano. On top of the piano is a hand-tinted enlargement of a snapshot of Veda and Kay.
    Bert comes in, takes off his coat, loosens his collar, and flops down on the sofa with a newspaper.

MILDRED'S VOICE (OVER SCENE):
> This was the kind of life I had. I hated it. Not because of myself. But because of my children—Kay and Veda.[18]

Mildred appears at the door of the kitchen, wiping her hands on her apron.

MILDRED:
> I pressed your other pants. I thought maybe you'd want to see McClary about that salesman's job.

BERT (sour; not looking up):
> It might be nice if you left me alone for five minutes, Mildred. When the time comes, I'll get a job.[19]

SOUND of doorbell ringing COMES OVER.

91.   FULL SHOT   LIVING ROOM
as Mildred hurries through to answer the front door. Bert pays no apparent attention aside from a flick of the eyes.

92.   EXT. PIERCE HOME   AT FRONT DOOR
with a neatly uniformed delivery man carrying an oblong dress box. The door opens, revealing Mildred.

MILDRED:
> Yes?

DELIVERY MAN:
> Package from I. Langlin. (He extends it together with the receipt pad.)

Mildred scribbles her initials and then closes the door.

93.   INT. PIERCE HOME   FOYER   (SHOOTING AWAY FROM DOOR)
as Mildred turns, looking over the package.

BERT'S VOICE (coming OVER):
> What's that?

Mildred looks up guiltily.

94.   FULL SHOT   FOYER
Bert is standing at the doorway that leads to the living room looking heavily at Mildred.

MILDRED:
> A dress. For Veda.

BERT (heavily):
> I thought so. Where'd you get the money?

Mildred starts toward the stairs. She gets up a few steps.

MILDRED:
> It was my money! I earned it.

BERT:
> That's right. Throw it up at me.[20]

MILDRED:
> I don't say half as much as most women would say with nothing but bills staring them in the face.

She continues on up the stairs.

95.   FULL SHOT   TOP OF STAIRS
as Mildred comes up and goes into the children's bedroom at the head of the stairs. Bert continues, from downstairs.

96.   INT. CHILDREN'S BEDROOM
as Mildred comes in and proceeds to unpack the dress from its box of tissue paper on the bed. This room, in odd contrast to the rest of the house, is pleasant and well furnished. Obviously Mildred has lavished money and loving care on her children's sleeping quarters. She hangs the dress up on the back of a closet door.

BERT'S VOICE (OVER SCENE from downstairs):
> Go ahead. Keep it up. Maybe you wouldn't have so many bills if you didn't try to bring up those kids like their old man was a millionaire. No wonder they're so fresh—and stuck up. That Veda! I tell you, I'm so fed up with the way she high-hats me, one of these days I'm going to cut loose and really clip her one . . .[21]

97.   STAIRWAY   PIERCE HOME   (SHOOTING UP AT MILDRED)
(MOVING SHOT)
as she comes out of the bedroom and starts down. At

Bert's line "I'm going to let her have one," which comes
OVER SCENE, Mildred freezes on the staircase.

MILDRED (in a deadly tone):
If you ever touch Veda . . .

Mildred's vehemence stops Bert cold.

98.   INT. LIVING ROOM
Mildred comes in, followed by Bert, who is watching
her closely as she crosses over to the fireplace. She is
cold with fury and pays no attention to him. After a
second's silence, he begins again.

BERT (watching Mildred's back):
The trouble is, you're trying to buy love from those
kids—and it won't work. I'm no bargain, but I make
enough to get by. But no, that isn't good enough.
Veda has to have a piano and lessons and fancy
outfits so she can sit up on a platform smirking her
way through a piece any five-year-old could
play . . .

MILDRED (hotly):
Veda has talent! You can ask the neighbors!

BERT:
Yeah? She plays the piano like I shoot pool. And
Kay. A nice normal kid that just wants to skip rope
and play baseball. But she's got to take ballet lessons! She's going to be a ballet dancer so you can
feel proud of yourself.

MILDRED:
All right, what of it? Why shouldn't I want them to
amount to something. I tell you I'd do anything for
those kids, do you understand? Anything!

BERT (quiet):
Yeah? You can't do their crying for them, Mildred.

Mildred Pierce

MILDRED:
I'll do that too! They'll never cry if I can help it.

BERT (shaking his head):
There's something wrong, Mildred. I— I don't know what. I'm not smart that way. But I know it isn't natural . . .[22]

The phone rings suddenly and she picks it up.

MILDRED (into phone):
Yes . . . ? Yes, he is . . . who's calling? (She smiles scornfully as she extends the phone to Bert.) It's for you. Mrs. Biederhof.

Bert takes the phone reluctantly.

BERT (into phone; evasively):
Yeah, Maggie? I—I can't talk to you now. I've told you not to— (He listens.) I can't talk to you now. Later . . . later, I said!

He hangs up the phone with a bang. Mildred sniffs at him.

MILDRED:
So the noble Mr. Pierce can't talk right now. He's too busy telling his wife that what's wrong with their married life is the way she treats the children . . .

BERT:
Maggie means nothing to me—you know that.

MILDRED:
I wish I could believe it. (Sweetly.) You'd better run right down there and apologize . . . she won't play gin rummy with you anymore. It is gin rummy, isn't it?

She walks into the kitchen, Bert following.

101

BERT (blustering):
> Now look, Mildred . . . don't go too far. One of these days I'll call your bluff.

MILDRED:
> You're not calling me . . . I'm calling you! You might as well know right now . . . once and for all . . . The children come first in this house.[23] I'm determined to do the best I can for them. If I can't do it with you, I'll do it without you.

BERT (livid with anger):
> Ah, now we get down to the point . . . you're just looking for an excuse to heave me out on my ear, is that it?

MILDRED:
> I never said—

BERT:
> I'm fed up. Let's *see* you get along without me for a while. (He starts out.) When you want me you know where to find me.

MILDRED (deadly calm):
> If you go down to that woman's house again, you're not coming back here!

BERT (between his teeth):
> I go where I want to go.

MILDRED (very quietly):
> Then pack up, Bert.

BERT (after a long glance):
> Okay, I will.

He starts out of the room, then suddenly stops.

BERT:
> The kids aren't home yet, eh?

MILDRED (a low voice):
> No—not yet.

BERT:
> I—uh . . . I don't want you to tell them I said good-bye or anything like that. You can just say—

MILDRED:
> I'll take care of it.

BERT:
> Okay, then. I'll leave it to you.

They look at each other for a long instant, each waiting for the other to speak. Neither will give in.

BERT:
> Good-bye, Mildred.

MILDRED (in a dull voice):
> Go on, Bert. There's nothing more to say. Just . . . go on . . .

She doesn't look at him as he goes out through the kitchen door, just stands there quietly, her head down. The CAMERA MOVES IN on Mildred. The tears are streaming down her face now.

> DISSOLVE TO:

98A. EXT. PIERCE HOME
A slick-looking convertible slides to a stop near the front of the house. Veda Pierce is fourteen, going on fifteen, at this point. She is carrying her music and wearing a sloppy-joe sweater and run-down, flat-heeled shoes that have reached the advanced stage of decrepitude so highly prized by high school girls. In the car is a young high school kid.

VEDA (stepping out of car):
> Thanks for the lift.

BOY (grandly):
> It was a pleasure.

99. FOLLOW SHOT
As Veda leaves the car and starts toward the house, Bert

drives through the driveway out into the street and away.

100. CLOSE SHOT   VEDA
Puzzled, she looks at her father's car as it goes by.

101. FOLLOW SHOT
as she crosses the street catty-corner and approaches a vacant lot down the street from the Pierce home. Some kids are playing softball in the lot and making plenty of noise about it. Veda is disgusted at the sight in a very ladylike way.[24]

102. FULL SHOT   SOFTBALL GAME
Playing center field, with her back to CAMERA, is a very determined young lady wearing boy's overalls, and with her pigtails tucked up out of the way. In common with the rest of the players in the field she is shouting advice to the pitcher and imprecations to the batter.

KAY (smacking her glove):
    Aw right—aw right—*here's* an easy out. (The batter in background fans.) At's a way . . . the big eye . . . come on, you lily . . . hit 'at ball!

The batter in background obliges with a long pop fly to center. Kay backs up for the catch, makes it, and heaves the ball back into the game.
    Veda comes into scene and seizes her sister firmly by the nearest protuberance.

KAY (indignant):
    Hey—what's eating you?

VEDA:
    You're coming home with me!

KAY:
    Awww— (She heaves down her glove.)

Kay accompanies her sister off the field.[25]

103. FOLLOW SHOT   VEDA AND KAY

as they walk along the walk on their way home. Kay alternately walks frontward and then backward, being very careful not to step on any cracks in the sidewalk, no matter what the effort costs.

VEDA:
Look at your clothes. Honest, Kay, I think you oughta take a little more pride in the way you look. You act like—like a peasant!

KAY:
Aw, pretzels . . . Whadda I care?

VEDA (primly):
You'll care some day, Miss Smarty. Wait till you get interested in boys.

KAY:
Aaah! I got over that when I was eight.

Walking backward, she turns sharply into the Pierce drive. Veda follows her.

DISSOLVE TO:

104. INT. PIERCE KITCHEN

Still crying a little, Mildred is just finishing writing Happy Birthday, Eddie on the cake. She wipes her eyes hurriedly as the screen door slams and the children come in.

KAY (giving her a kiss):
'Lo, Ma.

MILDRED:
Hello, darling.

VEDA:
Good afternoon, Mother.

Mildred gives Veda a peck on the cheek, as Kay becomes interested in the cake bowl.

MILDRED (peeling Kay away from the bowl):
How did your lessons go today, Veda?

VEDA:
I'm learning a new piece. "Valse Brilliante." That means—brilliant waltz.

MILDRED (dryly):
Does it, really?

VEDA:
I saw father go out.

MILDRED (in an immediate attempt to forestall questions):
Did you? Er—why don't you play your new piece for me, Veda? I'd certainly like to hear it.

VEDA (bored):
Oh, all right.

She walks into the living room.

MILDRED (to Kay):
Kay, just look at your clothes.

KAY (bored):
I know—I know—I should have been a boy.

105. INT. LIVING ROOM
Veda is playing her piece at the piano as Mildred comes from the kitchen to listen. Veda is more interested in her mother than the piano during the following.

VEDA (as she plays):
Father had a suitcase with him.

MILDRED:
Did he? (Still that effort.) That's a lovely piece . . .

VEDA:
Where was he going, Mother?

MILDRED:
> I— I don't know.

Kay has been taking an increasing interest in the conversation. Veda stops playing.

KAY:
> How long will he be gone?

MILDRED:
> It's hard to say. (To Veda.) Don't stop, darling . . .

VEDA (disregarding her):
> Is he coming back?

MILDRED (taking a stand):
> You might as well know . . . both of you. Your father and I have decided to separate.

For an instant nothing is said. Kay and Veda look at each other.

KAY:
> Is he mad at us?

Veda starts playing again.

MILDRED:
> It has nothing to do with you, honey . . . It just couldn't be helped.[26] (She looks directly at Veda.) I can't tell you about it now . . . someday I will, but not now.

Kay watches her mother and Veda with interest.

VEDA:
> If you mean Mrs. Biederhof, Mother, I must say my sympathy is all with you. I think she's distinctly middle class.

MILDRED:
> Please, Veda . . . It wasn't Mrs. Biederhof . . . It was just little things . . . but mostly about your dress . . .

Veda's entire attitude changes abruptly. Instead of bored impatience, her eyes shine with excitement.

VEDA:
My dress? It came!

She stops playing the piano and clatters out of the living room with Kay whooping along after her. Mildred is left alone. She starts to call after them, then changes her mind. Wearily, she starts taking off her apron.

106.   INT. GIRLS' BEDROOM
Veda has been removing what few clothes she wears, within reasonable limits, and now starts to put on the dress. Kay is lying on her stomach on one of the beds, watching critically.

VEDA (her voice muffled by the dress as it goes over her head):
It's awful cheap material . . . I can tell by the smell.[27]

KAY:
Whadda yuh expect? Want it inlaid with gold?

VEDA (emerging):
It seems to me if you're buying *anything* it should be the best. (She fusses with the dress.) This is *defin*itely not the best.

KAY:
Aw, stop, you're breaking my heart.

107.   FULL SHOT   STAIRWAY
as Mildred comes to the top, an expectant smile on her face as she goes toward the children's bedroom. The door is open.

108.   FULL SHOT   INT. BEDROOM
Veda is furious. She sniffs as she flips at the ruffles scornfully.

VEDA:
It's impossible. Utterly, utterly impossible.

109. FULL SHOT   MILDRED
at head of stairs. The smile is frozen on her face, and it
gradually disappears as she overhears the conversation
in the bedroom.

VEDA'S VOICE (continuing; OVER SCENE):
Look at it! Ruffles! I wouldn't be seen *dead* in this
rag.[28]

Mildred slowly leans against the wall, her eyes closed.
DISSOLVE TO:

110. OMITTED

111. FULL SHOT   BERT'S DEN   NIGHT
Mildred is seated at a desk, figuring intently. The desk is
spread with budget books, a bankbook, and various
legal-looking documents such as insurance policies,
mortgage deeds, etc. As CAMERA MOVES IN:

MILDRED'S VOICE:
It didn't take me long that night to figure out that I
was broke . . . dead broke. And with Bert gone, it
looked as though I'd stay that way.

112. CLOSE SHOT   MILDRED
as she finishes adding up the figures and subtracting her
debts. Then she stops wearily and starts putting away
the books and papers into various drawers of the bat-
tered desk.

MILDRED'S VOICE:
It was a warm night. I remember that. And far away
you could hear somebody playing the radio. But I
felt all alone . . . cold and lonely . . . For the first
time in my life I was lonely . . .

The CAMERA MOVES IN CLOSE on desk top, as Mildred
fingers various articles there. First a pipe, half-filled

with tobacco; then a wooden ashtray with Welcome to Niagara Falls burned into the wood; then in one of the drawers as she puts away a ledger she finds a limp and forgotten bow tie of the elastic variety.

MILDRED'S VOICE (CONTINUING OVER):
  —and there was so much to remind me of Bert . . . and how things used to be with us . . . and what great hopes we had . . .

Then, as she puts some insurance policies in the center drawer, her hand brushes against a gun. Almost furtively her hand returns to it and clasps the grip. She starts to lift it out. There is the sudden sharp SOUND of the DOORBELL RINGING.

113.   FULL SHOT   MILDRED
as she drops the gun into the drawer, closes it sharply, and twists the key. The DOORBELL RINGS again.

114.   FULL SHOT   DOORWAY PIERCE HOME   NIGHT
We cannot see the face of the man at the door, just his bulk. The door opens. We see Mildred inside, through the screen.

VOICE:
  Hiya, Mildred.

MILDRED:
  Hello, Wally.

115.   INT. PIERCE HOME   FOYER
Without awaiting an invitation, Wally pushes the screen door open, revealing himself, four years younger than we have seen him and a little thinner looking. He is wearing a straw hat, fountain pens and pencil in his handkerchief pocket.

116.   TWO SHOT   WALLY AND MILDRED
WALLY:
  Bert around?

MILDRED (coldly):
Not right now, he isn't.

WALLY:
Okay . . . I'll see him Monday. There's a little trouble over a mortgage. I thought maybe he could help
us out. Ask him to drop over, will you?

MILDRED:
If it's important you'd better look him up yourself.
He's—he's not living here anymore.

WALLY:
You mean you busted up?

MILDRED:
Something like that.

WALLY:
For good?

MILDRED:
As far as I know.

Wally starts into the living room. Mildred follows,
amazed.

WALLY:
Well, if you don't know, I don't know who does
know.

117.   INT. LIVING ROOM
as Wally comes in, looks around, making himself completely at home and throwing his straw hat on a chair.

WALLY:
You here all alone?

MILDRED:
No, I have the children.

WALLY (shrugs):
I never did mind being around you, Mildred.

MILDRED:
> You certainly kept it to yourself.[29]

WALLY:
> Me—I'm conscientious. (He flops on couch.) Not too much ice in that drink you're about to make for me.

MILDRED (eyeing Wally, sarcastically):
> Are you moving in?

WALLY (grinning):
> Maybe. Anyhow I'm not going to cry my eyes out because you and Bert are split up. I *like* the idea. (He looks her over carefully. Mildred feels a little self-conscious about it.) It makes me feel good.

MILDRED:
> I wish it made me feel good.[30]

She walks toward the kitchen. Wally gets off couch and follows her.

118.   INT. PIERCE KITCHEN
Mildred gets a half-filled bottle of liquor out of the kitchen cabinet. Wally gets two glasses from another cabinet.

WALLY:
> I've always been a little soft in the head as far as you're concerned.

MILDRED (dryly):
> You surprise me.

WALLY (continuing):
> This is on the level. Bert's gone. Okay. The way I figure it, maybe there's a chance for me now.[31]

MILDRED:
> Quit kidding an old married woman like me.

She hands the bottle to Wally, who starts to pour himself a stiff drink. Mildred goes to the refrigerator for ice.

WALLY:
I thought maybe you'd have a weak moment one of these days.

MILDRED:
If I do, I'll send you a telegram . . . collect.[32]

WALLY (pouring):
Say when.

MILDRED:
None for me. I'm not used to it.

WALLY:
You've got to get educated, Mildred. You've just joined the biggest army on earth . . . the great American institution that never gets mentioned on the Fourth of July . . . a grass widow with two kids to support.

As he tosses down the drink, Mildred starts to leave the room. As she passes Wally, he catches a tie-string of her robe and gives it a pull.

MILDRED:
Why don't you make an effort to grow up, Wally.

She goes into the living room. He follows.

119.   INT. LIVING ROOM

WALLY:
Why don't you forget about Bert?

MILDRED:
Maybe I don't want to.

WALLY:
You'll be lonely, Mildred. You're not the kind of a woman who can get along by herself.

MILDRED:
  I can try.

He takes her by the shoulders. She decides to stop things right now.

MILDRED:
  Wally, you should be kept on a leash. Can't you be friendly?

WALLY (grinning):
  I *am* being friendly.

MILDRED (fending him off):
  I mean it. Friendship is much more lasting than love.

WALLY:
  Yeah, but it isn't as entertaining.

He pulls her close to him and kisses her. She pulls away from him calmly but annoyed.

MILDRED:
  Cut it out, Wally. You make me feel like Little Red Riding Hood.

WALLY (laughing):
  Oh, I get it. I'm the Big Bad Wolf. (He is still holding her.) You've got me all wrong. I'm a romantic guy but I'm not a wolf.[33]

MILDRED:
  I know you romantic guys. One crack about the beautiful moon and you're off to the races!

WALLY (trying to put his arm around her):
  Is there anything wrong in that?

MILDRED:
  You'd better go now, Wally.

WALLY:
  No dice, huh? I'm sorry, Mildred. You know I

wouldn't pull any cheap tricks on you. You know that—

MILDRED:
Good night, Wally. (She hands him his hat.)

WALLY:
You don't want to see me at all?

MILDRED (opening the door):
I lost my youthful curiosity years ago. I said good night, Wally.

WALLY (going to the door):
Okay. Okay. Round one goes to Mildred Pierce.

MILDRED:
There won't be any round two.

WALLY:
We live in hope. I don't give up so easy.

Mildred closes the door after him.

120. FULL SHOT   FOYER
as Mildred comes to the door, and locks it. Then she goes back to the living room. The CAMERA PANS to:

121. FULL SHOT   LIVING ROOM   (SHOOTING THROUGH DOORWAY)
as Mildred switches off the light, and then comes back to foyer and starts upstairs, the CAMERA PANNING with her.

122. FULL SHOT   MILDRED   (SHOOTING DOWN FROM TOP OF STAIRS)
as Mildred comes up to the top, where the CAMERA PANS her to the door of the children's room. Softly, she opens the door.

123. INT. CHILDREN'S BEDROOM
At first it is completely dark, then a streak of light ap-

pears as the door is slowly opened. By the light, we see Veda's eyes, wide open in the dark. She's in bed. As the ray of light widens she turns her head toward the door.

124.   INT. CHILDREN'S BEDROOM   (ANOTHER ANGLE)
as Mildred comes in, leaving the door open.

MILDRED (whispering):
   Awake, Veda?

VEDA:
   Yes, Mother.

Veda reaches up and switches on the dim light between the twin beds. Kay is in the other one, fast asleep. Tears are glistening on her lashes.

MILDRED (as the light goes on):
   You'll wake up Kay.

VEDA:
   No. She's tired out. She cried herself to sleep.

MILDRED (pain in her voice):
   Oh. I'm sorry. Was it about father?

VEDA:
   Yes. Is he going to marry Mrs. Biederhof?

MILDRED:
   I— I don't know. I think you should be asleep.

VEDA:
   I've been thinking.

MILDRED:
   What about?

VEDA:
   I heard you and Wally talking.

MILDRED:
   You listened?

VEDA:
> I was awake.

MILDRED:
> Well—

VEDA (slyly):
> You could marry him if you wanted to?

MILDRED:
> I'm not in love with him.

VEDA:
> But, if you married him maybe we could have a maid and a limousine . . . and maybe a new house. I don't like this house, Mother.

MILDRED:
> Neither do I. But that's no reason to marry a man I'm not in love with.

VEDA:
> Why not?

MILDRED (levelly):
> Does a new house mean that much to you, Veda? You'd trade me for it?

VEDA (instantly and falsely contrite):
> I didn't mean it, Mother. I don't care what we have . . . as long as we're together.

She flings her arms around Mildred and hugs her. Mildred softens, and noticing it, Veda goes on slyly.

VEDA:
> It's just that there are *so* many things I—*we* should have, and haven't got.

MILDRED (tenderly):
> I know, darling. I know. I want you to have nice things. And you will. Wait and see. I'll get you everything. Anything you want. I promise. Now go to sleep.

VEDA:
How?

MILDRED:
I don't know. But I will. I promise. Now go to sleep.

VEDA (snuggling down):
All right, Mother.

Mildred stands up and looks at her tenderly, then leans down and kisses her cheek.

MILDRED:
I love you, Veda.

VEDA (impatient):
I love *you*, Mother. Really I do. But let's not be sticky about it.

This hurts Mildred, but she takes it calmly.

MILDRED:
All right, darling. Good night.

VEDA:
Good night, Mother.

As Mildred goes

DISSOLVE TO:

125.–127.   OMITTED

128.   INT. MILDRED'S BEDROOM   NIGHT
The CAMERA MOVES IN CLOSE as Mildred stares into space.

MILDRED'S VOICE:
I was sick and frightened . . . Over and over again in my mind as I lay awake that night I was saying to myself, "I've got to get a job. I've got to get a job."[34]

DISSOLVE TO:

129.   MONTAGE   (SERIES OF QUICK DISSOLVES)
OVER the following, we HEAR Mildred's voice and different interviewers' voices.

A. EXT. SEARS, ROEBUCK STORE   as Mildred goes in.

MILDRED'S VOICE (OVER MONTAGE):
> It wasn't as easy as I thought. I walked my legs off
> . . . until my shoes were so thin I could count the
> cracks in the pavement through them.
>> DISSOLVE TO:

B. MILDRED AT WICKET   The man shakes his head.

MILDRED'S VOICE:
> And always, everywhere I went, I heard the same
> thing—

MAN'S VOICE:
> Sorry—we need someone with experience.
>> DISSOLVE TO:

C. EXT. SHOE STORE   as Mildred goes in.

WOMAN'S VOICE:
> Sorry—need experience.
>> DISSOLVE TO:

D. EXT. DEPARTMENT STORE   Mildred goes in, past sign
marked Personnel Office.

E. CLOSE SHOT   INT. DEPARTMENT STORE PERSONNEL
OFFICE

PERSONNEL MANAGER:
> How can I give you a job if you have no experience?

MILDRED:
> How can I get experience if I don't get a job?[35]
>> DISSOLVE TO:

130.   FOLLOW SHOT   MILDRED   WALKING ALONG BUSINESS
STREET
She is apathetic and tired, too tired even to protest
when people bump into her, as frequently happens.

MILDRED'S VOICE (OVER SCENE):
> I was too tired, too sick at heart, to take the long trip
> back home without at least a cup of tea . . .
>> DISSOLVE TO:

131.   INT. RESTAURANT   (SHOOTING THROUGH WINDOW)
as Mildred comes along, looks at menu tacked onto
window, then starts into restaurant. The CAMERA PANS
her in, to where she is met by the hostess, Ida.

The CAMERA DOLLIES with Mildred and Ida to a nearby
table, where Ida hands Mildred a menu and stands waiting for her order. A waitress passes, then another. Still
another comes by with several orders balanced neatly
on her arm. Then, OVER SCENE we HEAR the SOUND of a
resounding slap.

WAITRESS'S VOICE (COMING OVER):
> I caught you, you dirty little crook!

ANOTHER WAITRESS'S VOICE:
> Don't do that again!

Mildred turns around in surprise. Ida hurries away.

132.   TWO WAITRESSES   (HER ANGLE)
They are standing near a table, glaring at each other.
Other patrons in the background stare curiously.

FIRST WAITRESS:
> I caught you red-handed, this time. Give it back.

SECOND WAITRESS:
> Go chase yourself. I didn't take your rotten tip. I got
> tips of my own.

Ida walks hurriedly up to the girls.

IDA:
> What's the trouble?

FIRST WAITRESS:
> She's been doin' it right along—stealin' tips. I seen
> her once but this time I caught her and—

IDA (low and tense):
Go into the kitchen. I said—go into the kitchen.

The two girls glare, then flounce sullenly out of the
SHOT.

Ida is trying to restore order without any apparent
success. Then the manager comes flying out of the
kitchen. Chris Makadoulis is a rotund little Greek who
dramatizes himself excessively.

CHRIS:
Ida. What gives?

IDA (indicating):
The rose of the Golden West has been lifting tips
again.

First waitress and second waitress are coming with tray,
arguing. In the background we see Ida trying to quiet
them down.

FIRST WAITRESS:
She stole ten cents off table eighteen, and just now
she stole fifteen out of a forty-cent tip.

SECOND WAITRESS:
I did not.

CHRIS (closing his eyes in patient resignation):
Please, girls, please.

FIRST WAITRESS (to second):
You're a fourteen-carat liar. Do you mean to tell me
that I didn't . . .

SECOND WAITRESS:
Don't you call me a . . .

CHRIS (indignantly):
This is not the boxing matches! You both go. You
are fired! (Screaming at one of the girls who starts to
show signs of saying something.) Please don't
make me for to lose my temper. Out! Out! Out!

His hat has become awry. He straightens it, as the second waitress flounces toward the kitchen with an insolent shrug. With the air of an impresario, Chris claps his hands and waves the other girls back to work, then turns and addresses the patrons.

CHRIS (very gracefully):
Please—I am most sorry that this should hoppen. If I had the time I would have a nervous breakdown I theenk. I would cut my t'roat from theese business . . . only I would get behind in my work.

He starts back for the kitchen as the patrons, somewhat amused, go back to their eating. Chris encourages them, as he walks to the kitchen.

CHRIS (to various patrons):
Please . . . eat. Be hoppy. Fill your stomachesez and take pleasure.

As he goes through the swinging door of the kitchen, we hear him address a final appeal in the direction of heaven. The doors close behind him. Ida goes back to Mildred's table.

133.   CLOSE SHOT   MILDRED AND IDA

IDA (shaking her head):
Shorthanded already, and this has to happen. Let's see . . . you wanted tea—

She turns to go. Mildred stops her.

MILDRED:
Wait—you need help? You've got a job open?

IDA:
Yeah—why?

MILDRED (getting to her feet):
I'll work. I want a job.

Somewhat surprised, Ida can only motion toward the kitchen.

IDA:
  Follow me.

As they walk along,

IDA:
  Did you ever work in a restaurant before?

MILDRED:
  No.

DISSOLVE TO:

134.   INT. LOCKER ROOM OF KITCHEN HELP
Ida brings out some uniforms. Mildred stands undecided.

IDA (noticing this):
  What size do you wear?

MILDRED:
  Fourteen.

Ida selects a uniform while Mildred slips off her dress. Ida remembers something, grabs up a bill of fare, and hands it to Mildred, who tries to look at it, remove her dress, and put on the uniform at the same time. Ida talks constantly.

IDA:
  Study the prices. We furnish the uniform but it comes off your first check. Three ninety-five. You get it at cost; keep it laundered. If you don't suit us, we charge you twenty-five cents on the uniform—that comes out of your check too. You keep your own tips.

Ida helps Mildred complete the finishing touches on the uniform.

DISSOLVE TO:

135.   SERIES OF MONTAGE SHOTS   QUICK DISSOLVES

  A. INT. KITCHEN   CLOSE SHOT   MILDRED AND IDA

IDA:

> I'm giving you a light station, see? Little booths against the walls. That's so you don't get no fours. Singles and twos are easier.

QUICK DISSOLVE:

B. MILDRED   CARRYING A TRAY OF FOOD
setting it down on table.

QUICK DISSOLVE:

C. INT. KITCHEN
as Mildred loads up a tray fast and starts by the carving counter. Chris stops her.

CHRIS:

> Look! You got spot on tray. (He rubs it off.) Don't get spots. All the time in restaurants you clean. One day only you not clean . . . Boom! You got cocka-roaches!

QUICK DISSOLVE:

D. CASHIER AND MILDRED
Cashier is talking to Mildred, who is looking wildly at her book of orders.

CASHIER:

> You gotta account for every check, see? Don't make no mistakes or it'll be deducted against you. You gotta pay for it, see?

Wearily, Mildred nods.

QUICK DISSOLVE:

E. MILDRED CLEANING TABLE
putting empty glasses and dishes on tray.

MILDRED'S VOICE:

> I learned the restaurant business.

QUICK DISSOLVE:

F. STACK OF DISHES
balancing on Mildred's arm.

MILDRED'S VOICE:
> I learned it the hard way. In three weeks I was a good waitress . . .

> > QUICK DISSOLVE:

G. MILDRED'S LEGS

MILDRED'S VOICE:
> In six weeks I felt as though I'd worked in a restaurant all my life . . .

> > QUICK DISSOLVE:

H. MILDRED CARRYING TRAY OF DIRTY DISHES
into kitchen.

MILDRED'S VOICE:
> . . . and in three months I was one of the best waitresses in the place . . .

135A. INT. KITCHEN (AT DOORS)
as Mildred enters and goes to the garbage bin, where she throws away a piece of pie. Chris comes into scene.

CHRIS:
> Whatsa matter this pie? Alla time you girls throw away pie.

MILDRED:
> The customer wouldn't eat it.

CHRIS:
> Why not he wouldn't eat it?

IDA'S VOICE (OVER SCENE):
> Because he's got good sense, that's why.

135B. KITCHEN ANOTHER ANGLE MILDRED, CHRIS, AND IDA

CHRIS (to Ida, deadly calm):
> You say my pies steenk?

IDA:
> Did you ever eat one, maestro?

CHRIS:
Don't changing the subject.

IDA (reaching for a piece of pie):
Here—take a bite—take a *big* bite. And then I'll
phone for a stomach pump.

Chris looks at her, trapped. He looks around. Everyone
is watching. He has to go through with it. He blusters.

CHRIS (preparing to eat):
It's a good pie. I make him myself. I am great chef.
Once I work for Rector. (He gulps a piece and goes
on.) And I make pies like you never tasted— (He
stops and then says mournfully.) It steenks.

MILDRED:
It's the crust that does it, Mr. Chris.

CHRIS (belligerent):
What you know from pies?

IDA:
She's a good cook.

CHRIS:
Hokay. You make pies for me. Thirty-five cents I
pay you. (He walks back to carving counter.) If they
no good—I no pay.

MILDRED (as she heads back into restaurant):
They'll be good.

135C.   TWO SHOT   IDA AND CHRIS

CHRIS (mournful):
Ida. Why you make me eat dot pie? You embarrass
me. (He shakes his head dolefully.) Someday I cut
my t'roat from this business.

Obligingly, Ida hands him a large carving knife and then
leaves.

DISSOLVE TO:

136.   CLOSE   ON SHELF
which is covered with pies.

MILDRED'S VOICE (OVER SCENE):
    . . . three months later I was baking six dozen pies
    a week for Chris. I was so busy I had to hire a
    woman to help me . . .

The CAMERA PULLS BACK SLOWLY to reveal kitchen. Every
available bit of space is covered with pies. The only clear
space is at the kitchen table in one corner, where
Mildred, floury and disheveled, is figuring something
on paper. Lottie, helping in the kitchen, is about thirty,
not too smart.

LOTTIE:
You need me anymore, Mrs. Pierce?

MILDRED:
Not tonight, Lottie. What time is it?

LOTTIE (shaking her head):
    Three o'clock again, I don't know how you stand it,
    Mrs. Pierce, honest I don't. I sleep all day, but you
    go and work in that restaurant just like you been
    sleeping all night—only you ain't.

MILDRED (smiling):
    It keeps *me* thin . . . (indicating bankbook) and *this*
    fat.[36]
                                        DISSOLVE TO:

137.   INSERT   (MONTAGE DEPT.)
Savings account book on the Glendale Saving and Trust
Co. The name is Mildred Pierce. The entries, which are
for small sums, total four hundred dollars.

MILDRED'S VOICE:
    I was doing all right. I was doing fine. I was able to
    send Kay to dancing school and Veda to a fine
    music teacher in Pasadena. Only one thing worried
    me . . .
                                        DISSOLVE TO:

138.   INT. PIERCE KITCHEN   DAY
Mildred has just entered, carrying the usual armful of
grocery bags. SOUND of Veda PRACTICING ON PIANO OFF.

MILDRED'S VOICE (COMING OVER):
. . . that someday Veda would come walking into
the restaurant. I was afraid she'd find out I was a
waitress . . . that I took tips, and was glad to get
them.

Rows of empty pie tins are scattered along a table, mixing bowls, etc. Lottie is stirring a bowl of batter. She
wears one of Mildred's waitress uniforms. Mildred
stops, looking at the uniform, surprised. Lottie turns.

MILDRED:
Where did you get that uniform?

LOTTIE:
Miss Veda gave it to me. She makes me wear it, in
case I have to answer the doorbell—

MILDRED:
Miss Veda.

LOTTIE:
She makes me call her that.

Mildred sets the bags on the table, turns, and exits.

139.   INT. LIVING ROOM
Veda is at the piano and Kay is going through some
dancing gyrations. The children do not stop as Mildred
enters. Kay has a heavy coating of lipstick and mascara
on and is trying to pretend that she is a very glamourous
young lady.

MILDRED (coming into the room):
Kay! What have you got on?

VEDA:
It's just some lipstick, Mother.

MILDRED:

Lottie, please take Kay upstairs and wash that goo off her face. Give her a good scrubbing.

Lottie takes the reluctant Kay by the hand and starts upstairs with her.

KAY:

Aw, . . . my face don't need washing. I washed it this morning.

Veda goes back to her piano playing. Mildred comes over to her.

MILDRED:

Veda!

VEDA (stops playing; bored):

Yes, Mother? What is it?

MILDRED:

Where did you find that uniform you gave to Lottie?

VEDA:

I was looking for a handkerchief—

MILDRED:

In my closet?

VEDA:

I looked everywhere else, and—

MILDRED:

All your handkerchiefs are in your own top drawer where they always are. What were you doing snooping around in my closet?

VEDA:

Really, Mother, it seems to me you're making quite a fuss about something which doesn't matter. If you bought the uniform for Lottie—and I certainly can't imagine who else you could have bought it for— then why shouldn't she wear it?

Her casual air of unconcern is just a trifle overdone. She gives herself away by the nervous gestures of her hands, from the piano to her hair, and back to the piano. Mildred seizes her by the shoulders and yanks her around.

MILDRED:
You've been snooping around ever since I got this job, trying to find out what it is. Well, now you know! You know, don't you?

VEDA (insolent):
Know what? (A pause.) Know what, Mother?

MILDRED (in a low voice):
You know that's my uniform.

VEDA (a bad pretense):
Your uniform?

MILDRED:
Yes. I'm waiting table in a Glendale restaurant. And you know it, now.

VEDA (throwing up her hands):
My mother—a common waitress!

MILDRED:
Yes. So you and your sister can eat and have a place to sleep, and a few clothes on your backs.

VEDA:
I'm really not surprised. You've never spoken of your people—who you came from—so perhaps it's natural— Maybe that's why father—

Mildred suddenly lashes out and slaps Veda across the face. Veda jumps up . . . nursing her cheek. Her eyes are frozen. There is an instant of silence. Veda clenches her teeth and lets out not as much as a whisper. It is Mildred who breaks. She begins to cry.

VEDA:

My mother. A waitress.

MILDRED:

I'm sorry I did that. I'd have rather cut my hand off.
I never would have taken the job if I hadn't wanted
to keep us all together. And besides, I wanted to
learn the business the best way possible—

VEDA:

What kind of business?

MILDRED:

Why—the restaurant business. I'm planning to
open a place of my own. (Veda perks up at this.)
There's money in a restaurant, if it's run right,
and—

VEDA:

You mean—you mean we'll be rich?

MILDRED:

People have gotten rich that way.[37]

VEDA:

Oh, Mother—I'm sorry I talked that way to you.
I've been horrible . . . all this time you've been
working so hard just for me—and Kay . . . and I've
been so horrid. I just didn't realize. Please forgive
me? Please.

MILDRED:

I'm sorry, too, that I slapped you so hard.

VEDA:

That's all right, Mother. I deserved it. I'll just try to
forget about it.

MILDRED:

It's all right, You've got pride, Veda. Never give
that up no matter what I say. I wish I had your
pride.

VEDA:
>I can't help it, Mother. It's just how I feel.

MILDRED:
>From now on things are going to get better for us.
>We'll have what we want. And all because of you.
>Every good thing that happens is because of you.

VEDA:
>Oh, you darling. I love you. Truly I do.

MILDRED (hugging her tenderly):
>Thanks, darling. Now, finish your practicing. I've
>got some work to do.

140.   INT. KITCHEN
OVER SCENE we hear Veda banging out, very loud, a
popular piece which no music teacher gave her for practice or anything else. It sounds triumphant, poorly
played, mostly noise. Mildred stands for a moment, still
holding her head bowed a little, her face grave, sad. As
the DISSOLVE BEGINS we hear Mildred's voice OVER.

MILDRED'S VOICE:
>I didn't know what to do next, but suddenly it hit
>me like a bolt of lightning . . .

DISSOLVE TO:

141.   INT. REAL ESTATE OFFICE
with a fairly successful air. The walls are covered with
land tracks, maps, etc. Wally Fay is at the desk, phoning
as Mildred comes in. He doesn't look up.

WALLY (gesturing toward the chair):
>Right with you . . . Hello, Max. I want sixty across
>the board on Paperboy in the seventh. Okay. (He
>hangs up phone.) Now what can I do you for?
>Mildred!

Mildred smiles at him as he comes around his desk to
greet her.

MILDRED:
Hello, Wally. It's nice to see you again.

WALLY:
Well—well—[38]using your gams all day hasn't hurt
'em any.

MILDRED (smiling):
This is all business, Wally.

WALLY:
You keep on saying no to me and one of these days
I'm gonna start thinking you're stubborn.

Mildred opens a briefcase she is carrying. It is filled with
papers.

WALLY:
What's all this?

MILDRED (looking at him directly):
Wally—I'm going to open a restaurant.

WALLY (curious):
You are?

MILDRED (firmly):
And you're going to help me.

WALLY (same tone):
I am? I mean—am I?

MILDRED (more firmly):
Yes.

WALLY:
I guess I am. What's the score?

MILDRED:
I've found the location I want. It's an old house that
hasn't been lived in for years from the look of it. It's
right on a busy intersection, which means a good
drive-in trade. I clocked an average of fifteen
hundred cars an hour . . . that's excellent, Wally.

And there isn't another restaurant within five miles.[39]

WALLY (impressed):
You sound like you know what you're doing.

MILDRED (getting to her feet and pacing in excitement):
I do, Wally. I figured it all out. I've studied the business. The big thing is to avoid waste and cut down the overhead. I'll serve a one-course dinner . . . chicken. Nothing but chicken. That way there isn't any waste. The leftovers go into soup and gravy and sandwiches . . .

WALLY:
It listens good.

MILDRED:
I need your help in getting this place. You know what the angles are—I don't. I want that house. Get it for me, Wally.

WALLY:
Who owns it? (He goes to his desk.)

MILDRED:
I don't know. But there's a For Sale sign on it, and the address is 35904 Glen Oaks Boulevard.

Wally takes out his real estate directory, and starts thumbing through it.

142. INSERT   REAL ESTATE DIRECTORY
which is a loose-leaf folder containing brokers' listings and pictures of the property involved.

WALLY'S VOICE (OVER SCENE):
Glen Oaks Boulevard . . . 35904. Ah, here we are.

He stops at a picture of the Beragon white elephant we saw earlier.[40]

143. FULL SHOT   WALLY
     as he turns to the back of the listing for information.
     Mildred comes into scene.

     WALLY (reading):
         Listed at ten thousand . . . will take eight, may-
         be less. Anxious to move property. (He looks at
         Mildred significantly.) Owned by Beragon Estate.
         (He consults credit book.) Beragon—Beragon
         Manor—Beragon Estate. (Reacting.) Well—well,
         whaddyuh know.

144. CLOSE   ON MILDRED
     who is tense with anxiety.

     MILDRED:
         What is it, Wally?

145. FULL SHOT   WALLY AND MILDRED
     as Wally closes the book, leans back in his chair com-
     fortably with a broad grin on his face, and starts dialing
     a number on the telephone.

     MILDRED:
         Tell me!

     WALLY (after he dials):
         The Beragons already lost two pieces of property for
         back taxes. It sounds like they're broke. Now watch
         Wally go to work— (Into phone.) Hello? Mr. Bera-
         gon, please. (His voice drips honey and good fel-
         lowship.) How-do-you-do, sir. This is Wallace Fay,
         of Fay Real Estate. Yes sir. I've been looking for-
         ward to the pleasure of calling you for quite some
         time. It's about your property on Glen Oaks
         Boulevard . . . I believe I've succeeded in interest-
         ing a client of mine in the possibility of a purchase.
         (He grins and winks at Mildred as he listens.) I
         thought possibly you might like to talk business
         . . . (He holds out the receiver toward Mildred,

laughing soundlessly. The voice on the other end is excited.) Well, how about this afternoon? Good. We'll come right down. Fay is the name. 'Bye. (He hangs up the receiver.)

MILDRED:
Well . . . ?

WALLY:
He's sweating blood already. Let's go.[41]

He grabs his hat and starts out. Mildred scoops up her papers and follows.

DISSOLVE TO:

146. EXT. HIGHWAY BY BERAGON HOUSE
as an automobile turns out of CAMERA and into the parking space by the Beragon beach house, revealing it. Behind it we see the ocean.

147. EXT. BERAGON BEACH HOUSE   ENTRANCE
as Mildred and Wally ring the bell. A houseboy comes and opens the door. They enter.

DISSOLVE TO:

148. FULL SHOT   ENTRANCE TO BAR
as Mildred and Wally, preceded by the houseboy, come down the spiral staircase. The CAMERA PANS to Monte Beragon, who is standing at the wide windows, looking out at the ocean. His back is to the CAMERA.

HOUSEBOY'S VOICE (OVER SCENE):
Mr. Fay, please.

Monte turns.

149. GROUP SHOT   (ANOTHER ANGLE)
as Monte greets Wally and is introduced to Mildred. Monte looks at Mildred with an appreciative air.

MILDRED (acknowledging introduction):
How-do-you-do, Mr. Beragon.

MONTE (smiling and indicating chairs):
  Sit down, please. Drink?

WALLY (grinning as he sits):
  I'm trapped. You've talked me into it.

Monte goes to the bar to mix drinks. He selects glasses
and dips some ice cubes from a bowlful and drops them
into the glasses.

  DISSOLVE TO:

150. CLOSE   ON NEARLY EMPTY ICE BOWL
  The CAMERA PANS to Mildred, who is looking out the
  window (ocean in background PROCESS), her back to the
  CAMERA.

MONTE'S VOICE (OVER SCENE):
  As I understand it, Mr. Fay, Mrs. Pierce wants to
  buy the house but doesn't want to pay for it.

151. FULL SHOT   BAR
  Wally and Monte are sitting on the sofa in foreground.
  Mildred in background.

WALLY:
  That's about it, Mr. Beragon. Mrs. Pierce will need a
  little time to get started. Once the restaurant is a
  success she'll be in a position to buy the property
  outright.

MONTE:
  I see. (He looks at Mildred.) That's a rather unusual
  proposition. How long would you need, Mrs.
  Pierce?

152. CLOSE   ON MILDRED

MILDRED (turning):
  One year, Mr. Beragon.

MONTE:
  You think you can make ten thousand clear?[42]

MILDRED (shrugs):
> If the place is successful, it'll be very successful. If it isn't you'll have your property back in better condition than it is now.

She turns back to the window, trying to hide her eagerness.

153. GROUP SHOT   WALLY, MONTE, AND MILDRED IN BACKGROUND

WALLY:
> Well, what do you say, Mr. Beragon? It's a gamble, but you can't lose much.

MONTE (thoughtful):
> I like to gamble, Mr. Fay. But I have to be sure of the odds. (He shakes his head.) And the odds are against me. No, I don't think I'm interested.

Mildred turns swiftly.

MILDRED:
> Please, Mr. Beragon . . . listen to me!

She comes toward them swiftly.

MILDRED:
> This is a gamble for me too . . . I'm putting every cent I have into this place, and I haven't much . . . believe me. I can't afford to lose any more than you. I've got all the information—exactly what it will cost—and how much I can expect to make. I *know* I can do it! I *know!*

For an instant Monte is thoughtful. He looks at Wally and then back at Mildred. Then he reaches a decision.

MONTE:
> Very well. It's a deal.

He gets to his feet. Mildred is smiling happily as they shake hands on it. Monte turns to Wally, who is grinning with self-satisfaction.

WALLY:
> I'll draw up the papers tonight . . . uh . . . there's one more thing. We'll need a predated transfer of ownership if that's all right with you.

MONTE (puzzled):
> You want the transfer immediately?

WALLY:
> Yes. We'll give you a note to cover the purchase, and you give us the deed. Very simple.

MONTE (shrugs):
> You take care of the details. (Turns to Mildred.) Well, Mrs. Pierce, how does it feel to be the owner of a white elephant?

154.   CLOSE   ON MILDRED
Her eyes are brimming with happiness. She takes a deep breath.

MILDRED:
> It feels fine. It feels wonderful.[43]

DISSOLVE TO:

155.   INT. CAR   (PROCESS)   ROOSEVELT HIGHWAY
as they drive off.

WALLY:
> Nice guy . . .

MILDRED:
> Very. Good looking, too.

WALLY:
> I didn't notice . . . I was too busy conning him out of that deed to the property.

MILDRED:
> What about it?

WALLY:
> It'll come in mighty handy when you go to the

wholesale houses and ask for credit. They don't
hear so good unless you can wave a property deed
in front of their pretty blue eyes.

MILDRED:
Oh—I never thought of that.

WALLY:
Leave the angles to your Uncle Wally. Now—
there's one more thing that has to be taken care of.

MILDRED:
What's that? (Something occurs to her.) I don't feel
romantic this afternoon.

WALLY:
Nothing like that. It's kind of serious, though . . .
about Bert . . .

156.–160.   OMITTED

161.   MILDRED AND WALLY   (ANOTHER ANGLE)   (FAVORING
MILDRED)

MILDRED (suspiciously):
What's on your mind?

WALLY:
You won't like this, Mildred. But you've got to get a
divorce—that is, if you want to open this restaurant.

MILDRED:
What has that got to do with it?

WALLY:
California has a community property law. Half of
whatever Bert owns belongs to you . . .

MILDRED (scornful):
What's half of nothing?

WALLY:

It works both ways. Half of anything *you* own belongs to Bert. You open a restaurant, and voom—every one of Bert's creditors will be hanging around with his hand out, saying "gimme."

MILDRED:

Is a divorce the only answer?

WALLY:

Yeah—why?

MILDRED:

He won't do it.

WALLY:

If he gets tough, you spring that Biederhof woman on him and he's got to give way.

MILDRED:

But there's nothing between them.

WALLY:

We can make it look as though there was. You don't ask him—you tell him.[44]

MILDRED:

But it takes a year to get a divorce in California, doesn't it?

WALLY:

You getting cold feet?

MILDRED:

No, but if it's no use, why do it?

WALLY:

It takes a year before your decree becomes final. But as soon as it's entered, the creditors can't touch you, and your worries are over.

Mildred is suddenly grim. This is a big decision to make.

MILDRED:

> I'll be seeing him next week—he's coming over to
> take the kids to Arrowhead for the weekend.
> Maybe I'll ask him then. I'll think about it.

WALLY:

> There's nothing to think about—no divorce, no res-
> taurant. It's like that.

MILDRED (stubbornly):

> I'll think about it.

Wally shrugs. They drive on in silence.

DISSOLVE TO:

162.   INT. LIVING ROOM   GLENDALE HOUSE

Bert is seated on the couch. Mildred places the tray of
drinks on the coffee table. Kay comes to the top of the
stairs and yells down.

KAY:

> Mother, Veda wants to know where her new bath-
> ing suit is. (Sees Bert.) Hello, Pa. We'll be right
> down. I'm all ready.

MILDRED:

> It's in the lower drawer of her dresser.

Kay goes into the bedroom.

163.   INT. GIRLS' BEDROOM

as Kay comes in, goes toward the dresser, and takes out
a package. Kay coughs from time to time. She has a
cold. Veda tries the new bathing suit to her body, just to
take one final look.

VEDA:

> I wonder if there are many boys up at Arrowhead?

KAY:

> If there are, they'll find you. Don't worry.

164.   CLOSE SHOT   BERT
He is seated on a chair in the living room of the Glendale
house. He looks pained and bewildered.

MILDRED:
Don't you see that it isn't a question of proving
anything to a court. It's whether they let me have
the property or they don't. And if I don't get a
divorce, they won't.

BERT:
Any way you look at it, it's unpleasant.

MILDRED:
I'm sorry, but it's unpleasant for me, too. Don't you
think I hate this just as much as you do? But it's got
to be for the children's sake. I have to think of their
future.

BERT:
Of Veda, you mean.

MILDRED:
All right, of Veda.

BERT:
What about Kay?

MILDRED:
Kay doesn't need thinking about so much.

BERT:
Kay is twice the girl Veda is and always will be. She
thinks you're wonderful.

MILDRED:
Maybe that's why I keep trying to please Veda.

BERT:
You'll always get kicked around, Mildred.

MILDRED:
Well, you ought to know. But I've made up my mind. I want a divorce.

BERT (getting angry):
I heard you the first time.

MILDRED:
And what's more, I'm going to get one.

BERT:
Not unless I say the word.[45]

MILDRED:
Bert, listen. I put everything I've got into this new restaurant. I've been working with the painters, carpenters, and electricians. Everything is starting to take shape suddenly. I've worked hard and long. I'm going to get this divorce.

BERT:
You think I'm going to be a nice guy and smack you in the face in front of witnesses so you can say in court that the defendant caused you great physical and mental anguish. (He shakes his head.) No, Mildred, no divorce.

MILDRED:
I'm going to file papers.[46]

BERT:
File away. I'll fight you all the way down the line. You *and* Wally Fay. And what's more—

He stops and turns toward the door as he hears the children clattering down the stairs.

165.   FULL SHOT   LIVING ROOM
as the children arrive at the doorway, carrying their suitcases.

BERT (forced cheerfulness):
Well, that was quick. Ready to go?

KAY (running to Mildred):
    'Bye, Ma.

MILDRED (kissing her):
    'Bye, honey. Have a good time. Be careful
    swimming—that water's awful cold.

Veda comes over and kisses Mildred distantly.

VEDA:
    Good-bye, Mother. (They kiss.)

Bert herds the children toward the door.

BERT:
    All right, let's go.

Mildred closes the door, cutting off scene, and leans her
back to it. The CAMERA MOVES IN to show the tears in her
eyes.

                                 DISSOLVE TO:

166.   LONG SHOT   EXT. RESTAURANT   DAY
The CAMERA MOVES IN establishing the parking space,
decorations, etc. The ground is covered with the debris
of construction: sawhorses, paint pails, etc. Two men
are hoisting Mildred's sign up into position. The CAM-
ERA MOVES in on a window of the restaurant, which is
being washed from the inside.

167.   INT. RESTAURANT
where Mildred is washing the window from the top of a
stepladder. Her legs are pleasingly evident.

MONTE'S VOICE (casual; OVER SCENE):
    It's moments like this that make you glad nylons are
    out for the duration.

168.   TWO SHOT MILDRED AND MONTE
Mildred turns, slightly startled.

MILDRED:
    Well, if it isn't our silent partner.

MONTE:
> I decided I've been silent long enough. I've come to check up on my investment.

MILDRED (gesturing with pride):
> How do you like it?

MONTE (who is definitely not looking at the restaurant):
> Delightful.

Mildred realizes that his interest is not confined to the restaurant and starts down the ladder.

MILDRED:
> Are you sure you're here to check up on your investment?

MONTE:
> Oh, absolutely.

MILDRED:
> This is going to be the counter. (She shapes it with her hands.) And over there will be ten booths. They can take care of four people to a booth—that's forty people.

MONTE (murmuring):
> Ingenious. Why don't you take the rest of the day off?

MILDRED:
> I'd love to, but I'm awfully busy.

CAMERA DOLLIES with them as they walk.

MILDRED:
> Now—in here is the bar.

MONTE:
> A bar—that'll be a novelty. (Meaningly.) I've got a bar in my beach house. Why don't you come down and see my ocean?

MILDRED:
> I've seen one. If you've seen one ocean, you've seen them all, I always say.

They are now at the entrance to the bar. Mildred points to it with a wave of the hand.

MILDRED:
> The way I figure it—why should they come to my place to eat and go someplace else to drink.

MONTE (agreeably):
> Very logical. Now, what about my ocean? It's getting colder. Let's take a swim before the sun goes down.

MILDRED:
> I wish I could go, but I've got too much work to do.

MONTE (persuasively):
> Come on.

MILDRED:
> You better look out, I might say yes.

MONTE:
> You know what might be a highly original thing for you to do? Just say yes right away like that.

Mildred is indecisive for an instant.

MILDRED (hesitantly):
> I really shouldn't.

MONTE:
> As you get older you'll find the only things you regret are the things you didn't do.

MILDRED:
> I hope you're right.

MONTE:
> I've got an errand to do and you probably want to comb your hair or something . . . Suppose I pick

you up at the corner of Colorado Boulevard and
Brand . . . (looking at his watch) in half an hour?

MILDRED (smiling):
All right.

DISSOLVE TO:

169.   INT. MONTE'S BEACH HOME   BEDROOM   ADJOINING BAR
CLOSE SHOT   BEDROOM CLOSET
filled with women's beach robes and bathing suits.
Mildred's hands are running over them. CAMERA PULLS
BACK to include her whole figure which is reflected in
the long mirror in the closet door behind her.

170.   ANGLE SHOT   (MILDRED IN FOREGROUND)

MILDRED (as she leafs through the bathing suits):
Are you hoarding bathing suits?

MONTE (from off-scene):
They belong to my sisters.

MILDRED (mentally counting the suits):
There's nothing like having a big family.

MONTE:
Yell if you need help with the zipper.

MILDRED:
I won't.

Monte disappears from the mirror, as Mildred selects a
suit.

MONTE'S VOICE (calling from off-scene):
How do you want your drink?

Mildred holds the swim suit against herself.

MILDRED:
Harmless.

She starts to disrobe.

DISSOLVE TO:

171.	SUN DECK OF BEACH HOUSE	(SHOOTING TOWARD HOUSE)
	CLOSE SHOT	COCKTAIL SHAKER
	being shaken vigorously by Monte's hands. Hands tip it
	up and pour liquor into two glasses, on portable bar.
	 As Monte picks up the two glasses CAMERA PULLS
	BACK. House door in background opens and Mildred
	comes out twirling a bathing cap. Over her shoulders
	she has a voluminous man's silk dressing gown, tied
	around her waist with cord. Her face lights up as she
	sees the ocean.

172.	ANOTHER ANGLE	(SHOOTING TOWARD OCEAN)
	as Mildred walks to glass window and looks out, almost
	unconscious of Monte.

	MILDRED (turning):
		I like your ocean.

	MONTE (extending glass):
		I borrowed it from the navy especially for you.

	She walks over to the portable bar.

	MILDRED:
		You certainly have a wonderful view.

	MONTE (his eyes on her):
		I wouldn't say that.

	MILDRED (laughs and looks around curiously):
		Do you live here all year round?

	MONTE (lightly):
		No. We have the old family mansion in Pasadena,
		complete with iron deer, a ghost, and a greenhouse
		with no flowers in it. I come down here in the
		spring.

	MILDRED:
		It must be lovely here.

	MONTE (shrugs):
		But lonely.

He crosses with the drinks.

MONTE (continuing):
> You know, Mildred . . . in the spring a young man's fancy lightly turns to what he's been thinking all winter.

MILDRED (dryly):
> It's a good thing California winters are so short.

He grins and hands her the drink. As she drinks, the robe falls back to reveal her bathing suit, and more important, what's in it. Monte's eyebrows reach for the sky. Mildred looks at him calmly.

MILDRED:
> No whistle?

MONTE:
> I'd need a police siren.

Under pretext of taking off the robe, he tries to put his arms around her. Deftly she slips out of the robe and his grasp and starts for the steps leading down to the water.

MONTE:
> Hey—where are you going?

MILDRED (looking back):
> Swimming—isn't that why we're here?

MONTE (glumly):
> I guess it is.

173. LONG SHOT   STEPS FROM SUN DECK
as Mildred comes down. On the edge of the sun deck we see Monte preparing to take off his robe. The CAMERA PANS Mildred to the water's edge. Monte comes PAST CAMERA to join her.

174. LONG SHOT   MILDRED
She runs out into the water and dives in flatly. Monte

follows. The CAMERA HOLDS on the water, flickering in the sunlight.

DISSOLVE TO:

175.   INT. BERAGON BEACH HOUSE   LIVING ROOM
as Monte puts a stack of records on the record player. He is wearing slacks and a sweater and a sports jacket.

At the fireplace, before a glowing fire, Mildred is drying her hair.

Monte gets the music started, then fixes a drink for himself from a decanter. Silently he invites Mildred to join him. She shakes her head.

MILDRED:
    You drink too much.

MONTE (shrugs):
    I do too much of everything. (Grins.) I'm spoiled.

MILDRED:
    Too many sisters. (She looks at her clothes.) They all seem to be my size.

MONTE (as he comes over and sits in a wing chair by the fire):
    Yes. I like them in your size. (Lifts his glass.) To— brotherly love.

He grins at her and drinks. Mildred smiles at him.

MILDRED:
    Thank you, Mr. Beragon. (Savoring the sound of it.) Mr. Monte Beragon. It's a very unusual name. Spanish?

MONTE:
    Mostly. But maybe a little Italian thrown in. But my mother's a real dyed-in-the-wool Yankee. That's why I'm such a self-controlled, dignified young fellow. (He makes a face.)

MILDRED (amused):
    And just what do you *do*, Mr. Beragon?

151

MONTE:
Oh, I loaf . . . in a decorative and highly charming manner . . .

MILDRED:
That's all?

MONTE (gently reproving):
With me, loafing is a science.

Mildred laughs, and throws her hair back. Monte is appreciative.

MONTE (murmuring):
You're very beautiful, like that.

MILDRED (smiling):
I'll bet you say that to all your sisters.

They both laugh.

176.   CLOSE   ON MONTE

MONTE (thoughtfully):
I'm not very impressionable, Mildred. I lost my awe of women at an early age. But ever since that day you first came here . . . I've thought of nothing else but what I'd say to you when we met again . . . (He stops and shrugs.) And now I can't say anything. You take my breath away.

177.   CLOSE   ON MILDRED

MILDRED (softly):
Do I? I like you, Monte. You make me feel—I don't know—warm . . . wanted. You make me feel beautiful.

178.   TIGHT TWO SHOT
as Monte leans forward, holding out his hand.

MONTE:
Shall I tell your fortune?

MILDRED:
> Can you?

MONTE (nodding):
> We Beragons come from a long line of teacup readers.

She stretches out her hand. He takes it and rises, pulling her up with him.

179.   FULL SHOT   MONTE AND MILDRED   (OUTLINED AGAINST THE FIRE)

MONTE (softly):
> When I'm close to you like this . . . there's a sound in the air . . . like the beating of wings. Know what it is?

MILDRED (breathless):
> What?

MONTE:
> My heart. Beating. Like a schoolboy's.

MILDRED (softly):
> Is it yours? I thought it was mine.

Leaning down, he kisses her. In the background the record player picks this moment to get stuck on a record, playing a single phrase over and over again. Mildred tries to pull away from Monte.

MILDRED (her mouth against his):
> The record—

Again he kisses her. The SOUND of the record keeps on.[47]

DISSOLVE TO:

180.   INT. GLENDALE HOUSE   LIVING ROOM   (2 A.M.)
CLOSE SHOT   ASHTRAY
which is nearly full of snuffed-out cigarettes. As we watch, a man's hand presses down another.

153

The CAMERA PULLS BACK to reveal Bert, seated at the telephone. He is agitated and unshaven, has his hat on. Beside him on the desk (or table) is a box in which has been hastily stuffed a child's bathrobe, slippers, nightgown.

BERT (into phone):
I'll wait five more minutes.

As he speaks there is the SOUND of a car driving up and Bert looks out the window beside him.

181. EXT. GLENDALE HOUSE MONTE'S CAR AT CURB
Mildred is getting out and Monte seizes her hand and kisses the palm.

182. INT. LIVING ROOM GLENDALE HOUSE
as before.

BERT (into phone):
Never mind. She's here.

He slams up the receiver, grabs up the box, rushes out of the room, and goes out the front door.

183. EXT. GLENDALE HOUSE FRONT WALK
Bert rushes down the walk to meet Mildred coming up, looking at the lights in the house.

BERT:
Where have you been?

MILDRED (a sudden fear):
What're you doing here? What's the matter?

BERT (distracted):
I've been calling you all day, until I thought I'd go nuts. Nobody knew where you were—

MILDRED (seizing him by the arms):
What's the matter, Bert?

BERT:
> It's Kay. She's sick.

Mildred glances toward the house as though Kay were at home, and makes a move to go up the steps to the house.

BERT:
> She's not here, Mildred. We came down from Arrowhead eighty miles an hour and there wasn't any time—

MILDRED:
> Where is she?

BERT:
> Mrs. Biederhof's.

MILDRED (stunned):
> Is it *that* bad?

BERT (miserably; nodding):
> Bad enough. It's pneumonia.

Mildred's hand flies to her mouth as she gasps in dismay.

DISSOLVE TO:

184. CLOSE ON KAY
as she gasps for breath. Her face is nearly covered by an oxygen mask (or nose tubing) but we can see that her eyes are glazed and her complexion mottled and cyanotic.
The CAMERA PULLS BACK to a FULL SHOT of the room, which is filled with the harsh, rapid, and painful shallow breathing that comes with pneumonia.
A nurse is engaged in keeping Kay from ripping off the oxygen mask. Dr. Gale, a small and efficient man, is taking Kay's pulse as he reads a thermometer.

185. OMITTED

186. CLOSE ON MILDRED
watching at doorway. Her face is lit by the glare of the
light from the bedroom and is sick with apprehension.
CAMERA TRUCKS AND PANS until it is shooting over her
shoulder.

Reflected in a mirror in the bedroom we see the doctor
preparing a hypodermic by the bed. He leans over.

187. FULL SHOT (SHOOTING ACROSS BED AT DOORWAY)
where Mildred is. As the doctor leans over Kay's upper
arm and plunges the hypodermic home, Mildred
winces.

KAY (a thin wail):
Mama!

Mildred involuntarily starts toward her. The doctor
waves her back. Mildred has to content herself with:

MILDRED:
Yes, darling—Mama's here.

188. CLOSE ON KAY
Her stertorous breathing is fast and loud in the silence of
the room. The SOUND of the hissing of the oxygen from
the iron bottles beside the bed is steady and loud.

DISSOLVE TO:

189. CLOSE ON DR. GALE
who has removed his coat. He is preparing another
hypodermic. Kay's breathing is still faster and shal-
lower. She is slowly drowning in her own secretions.

The CAMERA PULLS BACK to reveal Mildred, standing at
the door as before. Her face is haggard and drawn.
Suddenly her hand goes to her mouth, as there is a
break in the SOUND of Kay's breathing. Working
feverishly, the doctor jams home the hypodermic.
Mildred moves into the foot of the bed, her face in an-
guished suspense as she waits for the breathing to re-
sume.

Then again we hear the SOUND of Kay's breathing. It is very irregular now. The child's face is cyanotic (blue) to an extreme. As he straightens up from administering the hypodermic, the doctor catches a questioning look from the nurse. He shakes his head, as he hands her the hypo to refill.

Again there is a pause in the SOUND of the breathing. Mildred cannot help an involuntary moan, then is quiet, listening. The doctor works feverishly, feeling for Kay's pulse. He gestures savagely for the hypodermic, then stops as Mildred touches him on the shoulder and shakes her head, without taking her eyes off Kay. There is no sound of breathing. The doctor relaxes visibly. It's over.

The nurse turns off the oxygen bottle and the hiss of air slowly dies away, leaving the room quiet. Very slowly and with a set face, Mildred walks to Kay, reaches down and removes the mask, then kisses the dead little face and with a trembling hand, smooths the rumpled hair from Kay's cheek.

Steadily, she turns and walks out of the room, her face rigid. The doctor follows her.

190.   INT. LIVING ROOM   BIEDERHOF HOUSE
as Mildred comes out of the bedroom. The others in the room know from her face what's happened. Mrs. Biederhof wrings her hands and tears come into her eyes. Bert slams his cigarette to the floor then stamps on it heavily and turns away. Veda cries softly. Mildred turns to the doctor and looks at him blankly.

DR. GALE:
   I knew it was no use. But, we do everything we can. We can't give up.

MRS. BIEDERHOF (coming forward):
   I hope it was all right to bring her here instead of the hospital, Doctor . . . I thought it would save time.

DR. GALE:
You did the right thing.

MILDRED (a dead and level tone):
Yes. Thank you. Thank you very much, Mrs. Biederhof.

MRS. BIEDERHOF:
I'll fix you a nice hot cup of tea. (She exits.)

DR. GALE (as he rolls down his sleeves):
I'm sorry, Mildred. I brought her into this world. It seems hard that I was the one to . . . (He shrugs.) I'm sorry.

MILDRED:
Yes. So am I.

Veda walks over and kneels down by her mother.

VEDA:
Mother—

191. TWO SHOT MILDRED AND VEDA

MILDRED (wearily closing her eyes and leaning her head against Veda's):
I'll never forget it . . . never as long as I live. "Mama," she said . . . "Mama." And that's all. Then she was dead.

Mildred breaks down at last, sobbing bitterly.

MILDRED:
I loved her . . . I loved her so. And now she's gone. Oh, Veda! Veda. You're all I have now.

Desperately she clasps Veda to her.

MILDRED (tears streaming down her face):
Please, God . . . don't ever let anything happen to Veda.

FADE OUT

FADE IN

192. LONG SHOT   NEON SIGN   "MILDRED'S"
flashing on and off. The CAMERA MOVES in.

MILDRED'S VOICE (OVER SCENE):
>After that, there was only one thing on my mind
>. . . to open the restaurant and make it success-
>ful . . .

193. FULL SHOT   EXT. NEW RESTAURANT   NIGHT
It is in full blast. The drive-in bar at one side is crowded, and carhops are moving busily back and forth among the parked cars. Cars are driving in and out of the main restaurant parking space, and through the windows we can see that the restaurant is crowded. It is a cheerful scene of excitement and prosperity. The CAMERA MOVES in on front door.

MILDRED'S VOICE (continuing OVER):
>. . . and it was. For once luck was with me . . .

194. INT. RESTAURANT   AT DOOR
as Mildred ushers out a party of four. She is attractively dressed and carries menus and a folded tablecloth.

MILDRED (to the party exiting):
>Good night . . . thanks for coming . . .

They smile and murmur: "Delicious," "wonderful din-ner," etc. Mildred smiles at them, then says to the party of five:

MILDRED:
>I have a table for you now . . .

She starts toward rear, as man, woman, and guests fol-low her. The CAMERA MOVES with them.

WIFE:
>I told you we should have come earlier . . .

MAN:
    I didn't think the opening night . . .

MILDRED (over her shoulder):
    Oh, we've been jammed ever since the doors
    opened . . . right here, please.

195.   FULL SHOT   BOOTH
    Arline is just finishing clearing the table as Mildred and
    the guests come up. Mildred hands the guests a menu
    each as they sit down, then gives Arline the tablecloth
    and takes the tray of dishes.

MILDRED:
    I'll take these, Arline . . .

    She starts for kitchen, as Arline spreads the clean table-
    cloth in a white billow. The CAMERA FOLLOWS Mildred to
    where Ida is presiding over the cash register.

196.   TWO SHOT   AT CASH REGISTER   IDA AND MILDRED

MILDRED:
    It looks like we're in, Ida.

IDA (shuffling a packet of bills lovingly):
    That's what it says here. (She riffles money.) Isn't
    that a lovely noise . . .

    Mildred laughs and goes on toward kitchen, the CAMERA
    FOLLOWING. She pauses at a table by the window where
    Wally and Veda are sitting.

197.   FULL SHOT   AT TABLE   MILDRED, WALLY, AND VEDA
    Wally has just finished a drink and is in an expansive
    mood. Veda is very much dressed up.

VEDA (bubbling over):
    Congratulations, Mother . . . it's wonderful!

WALLY (businesslike):
    How would you like to sell?

MILDRED (smiling):
 No, thanks. I know a good thing when I see it.

WALLY (grinning back at her):
 So do I. And I see it.

The CAMERA PANS to

198. FULL SHOT   THROUGH FRONT WINDOW
 as the headlights of a car which has just driven in suddenly dim. We see Monte behind the wheel, illuminated
 by the restaurant lights. He sits there, his attention
 caught by the scene within. The CAMERA PANS BACK to

199. GROUP SHOT   MILDRED AND OTHERS
 as Wally rises to join Mildred.

WALLY (to Veda; indicating):
 Keep my seat warm . . . and get me another drink.
 I want to talk to your mother a second.

Mildred hands him the tray, which he takes reluctantly.

200. DOLLY SHOT   MILDRED AND WALLY
 as they go toward kitchen together, Wally carrying the
 tray through the crowd with some difficulty.

WALLY:
 Some mob, huh? Those postcards you sent out certainly paid off. There's nothing like direct advertising, I always say . . . 'Scuse me, lady . . .

This last is to a matron whose hat he has just knocked
over her eye with the tray.

201. DOLLY SHOT (FEATURING MILDRED)
 as she picks up two glasses from a table they're passing
 and adds them to Wally's burden.

MILDRED:
 What did you want to talk to me about, Wally?

WALLY:
It's about Bert . . . (Somebody walks between them.) He's coming here tonight.

MILDRED (faintly apprehensive):
He is?

WALLY:
Yeah. I talked to him last night . . . (Somebody else walks between them.) I talked to him, and he wants to see you . . . It's about the divorce, I think.

MILDRED (stopping):
What about it?

WALLY (shrugging):
You got me.

Mildred goes on again, thoughtfully. Wally starts after her, nearly knocking down a patron.

PATRON:
Watch where you're going, young man.

WALLY (politely):
Excuse me for living.

He follows Mildred through the door into the kitchen.

DISSOLVE TO:

202. INT. KITCHEN
Lottie is dipping halves of chickens into oil and plunging them into a frying kettle on the stove. Mrs. Whitley is just dumping a pan of rolls onto a wire rack. Pancho, a young Filipino boy, a piece of parsley tucked gaily over one ear, is washing dishes. Mildred is busily putting rolls on plates. Wally is helping himself to celery and radishes piled on glass dishes on the table.

MILDRED:
Never mind the dishes, Pancho . . . Wait on table.

PANCHO (pleased):
I am promoted?

MILDRED:
> You are. (Turning to Wally.) Give us a hand with
> the dishes, Wally. We're swamped.

Pancho slips off apron and hands it to a horrified Wally.

WALLY:
> Who—me? I'm an executive.

MILDRED:
> You're now vice-president in charge of dishes.
> Wash!

Glumly, Wally takes the sprig of parsley from behind
Pancho's ear and puts it behind his own.[48]

203. INT. RESTAURANT DOOR
Monte has just entered with a box of flowers. He steps
forward and flags Arline as she dashes by.

MONTE:
> Will you see that Mrs. Pierce gets these flowers?
> Just say they're from an old gypsy fortune teller.

Arline looks at him puzzled, then leaves, taking the
flowers.

204. INT. KITCHEN SLIDE
Wally is just taking a tray of dirty dishes and has paused
to look into restaurant.

WALLY (turning to Mildred):
> What do you know. Beragon just came in.

MILDRED:
> That's funny. He didn't say he was coming.

WALLY:
> What do you mean he didn't *say*? You been seeing
> him?

MILDRED (calmly):
> Don't let those dishes pile up.[49]

As she speaks, Arline comes in and tries to hand Mildred a box, but Mildred is busy dipping chicken.

ARLINE (with awe):
> They're orchids, Mrs. Pierce.

MILDRED:
> Put them in the icebox.

WALLY:
> Orchids! Say, what *is* this? (To Arline.) Who're they from?

ARLINE:
> He said he was an old gypsy fortune teller.

MILDRED (smiling to herself):
> Put them in the icebox.

They both look at her as she goes on dipping chickens.

205.   INT. RESTAURANT   ON VEDA
as she comes out of the bar, carefully balancing a drink. The CAMERA PANS her to the table where she and Wally have been sitting.
   Monte is sitting there. He looks up as she reaches the table and sets the drink down.

MONTE (rising):
> I beg your pardon. I didn't know this table was taken.

VEDA (sitting down):
> Oh, it's quite all right. We're *so* crowded tonight. Do sit down, Mr. Beragon. Please.

MONTE (amused; sitting down):
> You know me?

VEDA (with a grand air):
> Everyone knows *the* Monte Beragon. You play polo, go yachting, are an excellent hunter, and are seen with the most attractive debutantes in California. I read the society section.

Mildred Pierce

MONTE:
   So I gather.

VEDA:
   Perhaps I should introduce myself. I'm—

MONTE:
   Don't tell me. See if I can guess. Your hand, please.

VEDA (giving him her hand):
   Can you tell from my hand?

MONTE (a conspiratorial air):
   I wouldn't want it to get around but I come from a
   long line of fortune tellers . . . (Examining her
   palm with great seriousness.) Hmmm? Hm.

VEDA (greatly interested):
   What does it say?

MONTE:
   It says—that you look very much like your mother.

VEDA:
   Yes?

MONTE:
   And it says that—her name is—Bierce? Fierce? No—
   Pierce.

VEDA (with awe):
   That's wonderful.

MONTE:
   And it says that your name is . . . Veda. (He gives
   her back her hand, smiling at her.)

VEDA (looking at her hand from various angles, with
awe):
   Where does it say Veda?

MONTE (pointing):
   That line there—unmistakable.

Wally comes into SHOT.

165

WALLY:
Well—well, if it isn't Gypsy Beragon.

MONTE (grinning):
The very same.

Wally sits down.

WALLY:
Hey, Beragon, what do you say? Looks like it was a good investment after all.

MONTE (pleasantly):
Anything you did to this white elephant would be an improvement.

WALLY:
Smile when you say that.[50] By the way—I've got another little *business* proposition that might interest you.

Waitress comes with cocktail Monte has evidently ordered and sets it in front of him.

MONTE (carelessly):
Some other time. (Raising glass.) Well, here's to success!

Wally reaches over, takes his drink which Veda still has in front of her place, and raises his glass. Veda looks at them for a second and then raises her glass of water. As she drinks, her eyes are fixed on the palm of her hand.

DISSOLVE TO:

206.   INT. KITCHEN   (HOURS LATER)
CLOSE SHOT   TWO PLATES WITH VEGETABLES   HANDS
HOLDING FORK PUTTING FRIED CHICKEN ON EACH OF THEM
CAMERA PULLS BACK to show that it is Mildred holding
plates and Lottie putting chickens on them.

LOTTIE:
That's the last of the chickens. We just made out.

MILDRED (putting plates on table):
Now you and Clara sit down. You must be starved.

CLARA:
Thanks, Mildred. My feet are killing me.

MILDRED (starting for door):
I don't know whether I'm walking on my feet, or my ankles.

207. INT. RESTAURANT
It is deserted, except for Ida totaling at register and Pancho sweeping up. Mildred comes by the register. SOUND of jukebox at bar.

MILDRED (to Ida):
You must be dead.

IDA (showing money):
If I am—bury me with this. (Busy.) I told you we should have had a register that would ring up more than three hundred dollars.

Mildred goes to side of door and snaps switch, and exterior lights go off. Mildred goes to the bar, CAMERA MOVING with her. Behind it, Eddie, the bartender, is cleaning up. Wally is sitting on stool playing jukebox, and Veda and Monte are dancing nearby.[51] They stop and come over.

MONTE (to Mildred):
Your daughter and I have been getting acquainted.

VEDA (looking up at him adoringly):
Mr. Beragon promised to take me to Santa Anita Race Track.

MONTE:
Only if your mother will come along.

MILDRED (politely):
I'd love to. (Turning to Wally.) Wally, would you do me a favor and take Veda home?

VEDA:
Anyone would think I was a *child*.

MILDRED:
Well, you are. And it's way past your bedtime.

WALLY (aggrieved):
It isn't past *my* bedtime.[52]

MILDRED:
Please, Wally.

WALLY (grumbling):
Okay. Okay. This has been a big night in my life. I come out looking for an evening of fun and laughter—and what do I get—dishpan hands and a date with a Girl Scout.

He takes Veda's hand.

VEDA (to Monte):
I'm very glad to have met you, Mr. Beragon. Thanks for everything. (She bats her eyes at him.) I trust that we may meet again . . . very soon.

MONTE (amused):
Sure thing.

WALLY (over his shoulder; to Mildred as they start for main door):
Many thanks for a divine evening, Mrs. Pierce, and I trust that I shall see you in the not too distant future. (To Veda.) Come on, small fry.[53]

They go. Monte opens his cigarette case, offers Mildred one. She takes it.

MONTE (as he lights the cigarette):
That's a cute youngster of yours. I thought you had two.

MILDRED (after a pause):
Kay died.

MONTE:
> Oh—I'm awfully sorry. You should have let me know, Mildred. I *am* sorry.

MILDRED (voice trembles slightly):
> Let's not talk about it.

Monte puts his hand on her shoulder comfortingly.

MONTE:
> You've had tough breaks, but you're on your way now. I think you're going to make a go of this place.

MILDRED:
> I hope so. Well, I'd better get busy.

She gets up quickly and goes to the bar. As she passes end of bar, there is a flash from headlights of car driving up outside.

208. EXT. PARKING SPACE
The man in the car sits behind the wheel looking in at the scene, and we see from the flare of the match with which he lights his cigarette that it is Bert.[54]

209. INT. BAR
as Mildred picks up a cloth and begins wiping off the bar and piling glasses on a tray.

MONTE (seating himself on a stool beside her):
> Don't you ever do anything but work?

MILDRED (meaningly):
> *Somebody* has to.

MONTE (softly, as he takes her by the hand and pulls her toward him):
> Not all the time—there's a time for work and a time for— (He tries to kiss her.)

MILDRED (low tone):
> Monte, don't! Not here.

MONTE:
> Why not? We're all alone. And I've waited all evening—a lifetime.

He leans over and kisses her. The CAMERA PANS AWAY TO:

210.   FULL SHOT   AT DOOR   BERT
He looks at them, then closes the door, deliberately being noisy.

211.   FULL SHOT   (SHOOTING PAST MILDRED AND MONTE)
as they break apart, startled.

MILDRED:
> Bert!

Bert comes forward. Mildred goes to meet him.

BERT (heavily):
> I didn't mean to bust in like this . . .

MILDRED:
> That's all right. (To Monte.) This is my er—husband. (To Bert.) This is Mr. Beragon. Monte Beragon.

BERT (levelly):
> I've heard a lot of things about you, Mr. Beragon.

MONTE (lightly):
> Nice things, I hope.

BERT (disregarding him):
> If you don't mind . . . I'd like to talk to Mildred.

Monte turns away and goes to the bar, his back turned toward them.

MILDRED:
> What is it, Bert?

BERT (fumbling for words; he's completely miserable):
It'll only take a minute. It's—it's— (A rueful laugh.)
Funny—it's hard to say. Harder than I thought.

MILDRED (with quick sympathy, as she reaches out to
touch his arm):
Bert—

BERT (avoiding her touch and not looking at her):
It's about the divorce. You can have it. (Then he
goes on quickly, looking at the floor.) When I
walked out on you that time, I told you to see if you
could get along without me. I didn't think you
could. When you asked me for the divorce—

MILDRED:
Bert. Please—

BERT:
I still didn't think you could make it alone. Now I
know better. You're doing all right, Mildred. You're
doing fine. (He smiles shyly at her then looks down
again.) You don't need *me* anymore.

MILDRED (softly):
Bert—I never thought it would end like this.

BERT (looking at her):
Neither did I. I'm sorry.

MILDRED:
So am I.

BERT (more briskly):
Well, anyhow—that's that. That's what I came to
say and now it's said. I just want you to know I
wish you all the luck in the world.

MILDRED (her hand on his; this time he doesn't avoid it
but puts his hand over hers):
Thanks. Thanks a lot, Bert.

212. FULL SHOT   ANOTHER ANGLE   (TO INCLUDE MONTE AT THE BAR)
Monte has mixed some drinks. Now he walks over to Mildred and Bert with them.

MONTE:
> I think this calls for a drink—

He hands Mildred a drink and stands beside her as he extends the other one toward Bert.

MONTE (pleasantly):
> In the Beragon family, there's an old Spanish proverb . . . "One man's poison is another man's meat."

Bert looks at him for an instant, then all the misery in him suddenly comes to the surface. Savagely, he knocks the drink from Monte's hand.

213. CLOSE   ON FLOOR
as the glass smashes there. The pieces slowly come to rest.[55]

DISSOLVE TO:

214. FULL SHOT   INT. PETERSON'S OFFICE
The CAMERA MOVES IN to a CLOSE SHOT of Mildred, who is staring ahead.

MILDRED:
> I was in love with him. I knew it for the first time that night the restaurant opened. Now he's dead and it's over, and I'm not sorry.

She turns her head toward Inspector Peterson.

215. TWO SHOT   PETERSON AND MILDRED
Peterson is sitting behind his desk doodling on a pad of paper as he listens to Mildred.

MILDRED:
> He wasn't worth it.

PETERSON (who doesn't look up):
> That may be. Whoever put the kill on him evidently
> agreed with you. But you still haven't given us one
> good reason why your first husband here— (indi-
> cating) wasn't the murderer. In fact, Mrs. Bera-
> gon— (he gets up and walks around his desk)
> you've given us a very good reason why Pierce *did*
> kill Beragon. Look at it our way. (He ticks off on his
> fingers.) One—Beragon was killed with Pierce's
> gun. Two—Pierce can't account for his movements
> at the time the murder was committed. Three— (he
> leans toward her) he had a motive, Mrs. Beragon!
> You've just given it to us. Jealousy!

216.   FULL SHOT   PETERSON'S OFFICE
as the door opens and Ed comes in with some papers.
Peterson breaks off what he's saying and looks up at Ed.

ED:
> This report just came in from the chemist . . .
> thought you'd want to see it.

Ed crosses and hands a sheaf of papers to the inspector,
who glances carelessly at the report, then stiffens and
looks up keenly at Ed.

PETERSON:
> He's sure?

ED (shrugging):
> You know Charley. He don't like to make mistakes.

Peterson glances swiftly at Mildred who seems apprehensive, then picks up the pad from his desk and
scribbles something on it rapidly. He rips off the piece of
paper and shows it to Ed.

PETERSON:
> Right away.

ED:
> Okay.

Ed turns and goes out. Peterson crumples the piece of paper and throws it into the wastebasket. Then he turns to Mildred again. When he speaks his voice is soft and predatory.

PETERSON:
> Mrs. Beragon . . . we have some new information here— (he indicates report) that puzzles us a little.[56] For instance—your business manager— (he consults the report) Ida Corwin. She tells us that you called her at approximately eleven forty-five in the evening and asked where Mr. Beragon was. You seemed quite upset, according to her statement.

MILDRED:
> It—it was a business matter.

PETERSON (smiling as though convinced):
> I see. There was nothing wrong when you called?

MILDRED:
> No.

PETERSON (genially):
> Mrs. Beragon . . . occasionally we run across a witness who won't tell us what we want to know except under pressure . . . like Wally Fay, for example. His story was a little thin, and my men have been "talking" to him . . . Suddenly he remembers a rather interesting piece of information. (Suddenly sharp.) Why did you take him to the beach house?

MILDRED:
> I—

PETERSON (never allowing her to speak):
> Did you know that Beragon was lying there dead in the house?

MILDRED:
> No! I—

PETERSON:

> Then you *were* at the beach house this evening. Why didn't you tell us before? And why did you run away from the house? Wasn't it because you knew Beragon was there—dead? And if you *did* know, why were you trying to pin the murder on Fay—why? (Then very gently.) I think you'd better tell us the truth now.

MILDRED (as though confirming what he already knows):

> I did it. I killed him.

PETERSON (flatly):

> Why? Your restaurant was a success . . . You were in love with Beragon . . . What happened to all that?

217. CLOSE ON MILDRED

as she gazes into the past.

MILDRED (a dull tone):

> The restaurant was a greater success than I knew that night . . . the profits were enormous. In a few months I opened another place . . . at Laguna Beach . . . then I started a chain. In three years I had built five restaurants.

> > DISSOLVE TO:

218. QUICK MONTAGE

showing busy restaurants from various angles, interior and exterior. Prominently featured are the distinctive signs "Mildred's" and the busy cash registers. In the interior shots we generally see Mildred, watching and supervising. Ida is also prominent.

MILDRED'S VOICE (OVER SCENE):

> Everywhere you went I had a restaurant . . . they made money. Everything I touched turned into money . . . and I needed it. I needed it for Veda.

219.   FULL SHOT   MONTE
as he dismounts from polo pony, flushed with exertion
and triumph. He goes toward the stands where he is
congratulated by Veda—an expensively dressed Veda.
A photographer rushes up and takes their picture, the
same one we've seen before.

MILDRED'S VOICE (continuing OVER):
    . . . she was becoming a young lady . . . with ex-
    pensive tastes.

220.   FULL SHOT   NIGHTCLUB   (PEOPLE DANCING)
The CAMERA PANS UP from the floor to reveal a superbly
gowned young lady with a beautiful figure. It's Veda,
dancing with Ted Forrester.

MILDRED'S VOICE (continuing OVER):
    She was beautiful and filled with the lovely grace of
    youth. Veda was growing up.

Veda smiles over Ted's shoulder, and waves to off-
scene. The CAMERA PANS to where she is waving, revealing Mildred and Monte at a table near the floor. Mildred
smiles back at Veda. Monte is fiddling with his glass.
The CAMERA MOVES in on them.

221.[–222.] TWO SHOT   MILDRED AND MONTE

MILDRED (watching Veda):
    That Ted Forrester is a nice-looking boy, isn't he?
    Veda likes him.

MONTE:
    Who wouldn't? He's got a million dollars.

MILDRED:
    What's the matter, Monte?

MONTE:
    Oh—it's nothing. (A forced laugh.) I've run out of
    jokes, that's all.

MILDRED (quietly insistent):
What is it, Monte? Tell me.

MONTE:
I—uh—I've had a little bad luck lately. I can't afford
many more evenings like this.

MILDRED:
Do you need money?

MONTE (embarrassed):
No—no. It isn't that.

MILDRED:
I think you do.

Mildred holds her purse under the table and removes a
sheaf of bills.

MONTE:
Don't do that. Please, Mildred.

223.   CLOSE   ON THEIR HEADS
as she presses the money on him.

MILDRED'S VOICE:
You've been very good to us, Monte. Please—take
it.

224.   CLOSE   ON MONTE
who is flushed and embarrassed. He looks this way and
that surreptitiously to see if anyone has noticed.

MONTE:
Well—all right. If you say so. I'll pay it back.

225.   TWO SHOT   MILDRED AND MONTE
as Mildred leans back and sips her drink.

MONTE:
I want it distinctly understood that it's only a loan.

MILDRED:
Any way you want it. Long as we're friends.

She smiles at him. He smiles back, most charmingly.
DISSOLVE TO:

226.   CLOSE   ON SHEAF OF BILLS
from various places in and around Hollywood. They are
being turned over one by one, by someone who gets
increasingly agitated by them.

MILDRED'S VOICE (OVER SCENE):
That's how it began. At first it bothered Monte to
take money from me. Then it became a habit with
him . . .

The CAMERA PULLS BACK to reveal Wally, who has been
turning over the bills in front of Mildred, who is sitting
behind her desk in the Beverly Hills restaurant.

WALLY (bitterly):
Total . . . fourteen hundred eighty dollars and
twenty-nine cents . . . in six months. What's the
big idea?

MILDRED:
We owe him a great deal.

WALLY:
The restaurant was paid off a year ago. You don't
owe him a cent. (She starts to speak; he stops her.)
Now listen, Mildred. I agreed to manage this business for you . . . so far I've done all right. But
keeping Monte Beragon in monogrammed shirts
isn't my idea of business.[57] Anyhow it isn't what
I've been working for, I'll tell you that.

MILDRED:
What have you been working for?

WALLY:
I had an idea you might change your mind about
me . . . maybe I made a mistake.

MILDRED (a level tone):
You did, Wally.

WALLY:
Okay. I helped you get these restaurants . . . maybe I can help you lose 'em.

MILDRED:
Threats, Wally?

WALLY:
You figure it out.

MILDRED:
I know what I'm doing.

WALLY:
You're making a mistake, Mildred. This guy Beragon is no good. He'll bleed you dry . . .

MILDRED (a level tone):
I happen to be in love with him.

WALLY (bitterly):
Okay. Now I know where I stand.

MILDRED:
That's right—now you know.

For an instant Wally looks at her, then turns and stalks out. The CAMERA PANS TO:

227.   FULL SHOT   AT DOOR
As Wally goes out, he passes Ida coming in with some papers.[58] She looks at him curiously. The CAMERA PANS Ida over to Mildred's desk. Mildred is standing with her back to the room, looking out the window.

IDA (to Mildred):
Laughing Boy seems slightly burned at the edges. What's *eating* him?

MILDRED (turning):
A small green-eyed monster.

IDA:

> Jealous? Doesn't sound like Wally. (Explaining.) No
> profit in it . . . and *there* is a guy who loves a dol-
> lar.[59]

She puts the papers she carries on the desk. With them
is a bunch of car keys.

MILDRED (still at the window):
> What's that for?

IDA (dryly):
> A little eighteen-hundred-dollar birthday present
> for Miss Veda.

MILDRED:
> The car. It came.

IDA:
> Yes. It's that shiny blue thing a block and a half long
> . . .

She indicates the window that overlooks the parking
space. Mildred looks out.

228. LONG SHOT (SEEN THROUGH WINDOW) BUICK
CONVERTIBLE

MILDRED'S VOICE (OVER SCENE):
> Do you think she'll like it, Ida?

229. MED. CLOSE ON IDA
at desk, as she dips fountain pen.

IDA:
> If she doesn't she oughta have her head examined
> for holes. Here—you have to sign this . . . in
> blood.

Mildred goes to the desk and starts signing receipt. Ida
is oddly nervous and hesitant. Mildred notices.

IDA:

Uh . . . look, Mildred. This is none of my business . . .

MILDRED:

If it's about Monte, I agree with you.

IDA:

It's about Veda. She's been borrowing money.

MILDRED (this is a surprise):
From whom?

IDA:

Everybody that would give her any. The waitresses mostly.

MILDRED:
Doesn't she pay them back?

IDA (shakes her head):
They've been afraid to say anything . . . or turn her down. You know how it is.

MILDRED (grimly):
Tell them to come to me, and I'll see that they're paid back. (She busies herself with some papers, then slams the palm of her hand down on them angrily.)

IDA:

I'm sorry. I had to tell you, Mildred. I don't blame her so much . . . a couple of times Monte was with her, and—

MILDRED:
Monte! Always Monte![60]

Through the glass windows behind Mildred's desk we have seen a car pull into the parking space. Now Monte and Veda come in through the side door. Mildred gathers papers together.

VEDA (sweeping in):
> Hello, Ida . . . hello, Mother darling. Working hard?

MILDRED (handing papers to Ida):
> Hello, Veda . . . Monte. This won't take much longer . . .

MONTE (sitting down in an easy chair):
> I hope not . . . if there's one thing I can't stand it's watching people work— (He shudders delicately.)

IDA:
> Your mother must have been frightened by a callous . . .

Mildred gathers up the last of the papers, puts them into a folder, and gives them to Ida. Veda plunks down on the corner of the desk and produces a cigarette case.

MILDRED (to Ida):
> I guess that's all.

Ida has checked the statements given to her by Mildred.

IDA:
> One missing. (Then, to Veda.) You're sitting on the statement from Laguna Beach . . .

Ida pries the papers out from under Veda, who isn't too pleased.

VEDA (fishing for a cigarette):
> That's what I like about you, Ida. You're so informal . . . so delightfully provincial . . .

IDA (sweet):
> I like you too . . .[61]

MILDRED (to Veda who has just accepted a light from Monte):
> When did you start smoking?

VEDA (airily):

> Just the other day. Ted Forrester [62] gave me this for my birthday— (indicating case) and after all, I couldn't hurt the poor boy by not using it. I mean, that would have been dreadfully recherche, n'est-ce pas?

MILDRED:

> I suppose so— Here—this is for your birthday too. I hope you like it . . .

She tosses the key ring to Veda, who doesn't understand at first. Then she gasps with delight.

VEDA:

> Oh, Mother! A car! Where is it?

MILDRED:

> Look out the window . . .

Veda walks quickly to the window. Mildred and Monte follow, CAMERA WITH THEM. Veda looks out and gasps, then turns and flings her arms around Mildred.

VEDA:

> Oh, Mother! You darling!

MONTE:

> Hey—how about me, lady? I picked it out.

VEDA (her arms around him):

> Oh, Monte . . . it's the nicest present I ever got. You're sweet . . . really you are.

Mildred is a trifle put out. Suddenly the present seems to have emanated from Monte. Veda takes Monte by the hand and drags him toward the French window.

VEDA:

> Let's go for a drive . . .

MONTE (agreeably):

> Nothing I'd like better . . .

MILDRED (her voice suddenly harsh):
  Wait, Monte! (Then as they all look at her.) I—I
  want to talk to you.

MONTE:
  Oh, all right. (To Veda.) Run along, and dent your
  fenders.

VEDA (carelessly):
  All right—sorry I can't stay longer, but I have a date
  with Ted. 'Bye now.

Veda waves an offhand kiss to Mildred and exits
through the window.

230.   LONG SHOT   (THROUGH WINDOW)
        as Veda runs to the car and climbs in. She tries the
        wheel excitedly, then starts the car and drives off furi-
        ously, blaring her horn and waving.[63]
            CAMERA PULLS BACK from window, to REVEAL Mildred
        and Monte turning away. Monte is amused by Veda.
        Mildred's face is set. Ida is at the desk, with the papers.
        She starts for the door.

MONTE (to Ida):
  Finished for the day?

IDA:
  Yeah. (As she prepares to exit.) Don't look now,
  junior . . . but you're standing under a brick wall.

MONTE (puzzled):
  I don't get it.

IDA:
  You will.

She goes out. Monte shrugs in perplexity, then goes
over to Mildred, puts his arms around her, and tries to
kiss her.

MILDRED (breaking away):
  Don't.

MONTE:
What's the matter?

Mildred turns to face him.

MILDRED:
I want you to do me a favor, Monte . . .

MONTE:
Sure. What?

MILDRED:
Stay away from Veda.

MONTE:
Why? What's wrong with me? Have I suddenly
sprouted two heads?

MILDRED:
I just don't want you to take her out so much, that's
all. (Monte laughs.) And it isn't funny.

MONTE (still amused):
You're jealous.[64] That's what it is. (Seriously.)
Mildred—she's just a kid.

MILDRED (snapping):
That's the point, Monte! She's only seventeen years
old . . . and she's rotten spoiled.

MONTE (getting irritated):
Don't blame that on me.

MILDRED:
I've worked long and hard, Monte . . . trying to
give Veda the things I never had. I've done without a lot of things—including happiness sometimes—because I wanted her to have everything.
And now I'm losing her. She's drifting away from
me . . . she hardly talks to me anymore except to
ask for money . . . or poke fun at me in French
because I work for a living.

MONTE:

Oh, all kids are thoughtless at her age . . .

MILDRED:

I don't like it, Monte! And I blame it on the way she's been living.[65]

MONTE (annoyed acceptance):

All right, all right . . . I won't take her out anymore. How's that?

MILDRED:

That's fine.

MONTE:

But I'm warning you, Mildred . . . I don't think you know Veda very well . . . She's not like you . . . You'll never make a waitress out of *her*.

MILDRED:

You look down on me because I work. You always have. All right, I work. I cook food and sell it. And I make a profit on it . . . which I might point out you're not too proud to share with me.

Monte looks at her, with hatred in his glance.

MONTE:

Yes, I take money from you, Mildred. But I flatter myself that I give value for value received . . .

MILDRED (a softer tone):

Monte—why can't you be different? We could get married, and you could manage the restaurants . . .

MONTE:

No, thanks. I don't like kitchens . . . or cooks . . . they smell of grease.

MILDRED (furious):

You don't mind the money though, do you? I don't notice you shrinking away from a fifty-dollar bill because it smells of grease . . .

Mildred Pierce

MONTE:
Take it easy, Mildred . . .

MILDRED (whirling on him):
I won't! I've been in love with you for a long time, Monte . . .[66] but there's no point in going on like this. You're interfering with my life . . . and my business . . . and worst of all, you're interfering with my plans for Veda. I won't stand for it.

MONTE:
I always knew that someday we'd come to this particular moment in the scheme of things . . .

MILDRED:
Monte—

MONTE (almost sadly):
Nothing is free, Mildred. Not even what we do. Sooner or later the bill comes 'round, and it has to be paid. You want Veda, your business, and a nice quiet life . . . and the price of all that is me. (A pause.) You can go back to making pies now, Mildred. We're through.

For an instant Mildred is motionless. Then she goes to her desk, and fumbles in a drawer for her checkbook.

MILDRED (making out a check):
You've been very good to us, Monte . . . I know you've had expenses taking Veda out . . . I don't know how much we owe you, but— (holding out the check) if this isn't enough, let me know.

Monte takes the check, with a rueful grin. He doesn't even look at the amount, but folds it very carefully. Then he goes to the window.

MONTE (at the window):
I've always wondered how it felt to take a tip, Mildred. (He waves check.) Thanks. Mark our account "paid in full."

He goes out. The CAMERA MOVES in on Mildred, whose eyes are brimming with tears as she watches Monte go to his car.[67]

231.   LONG SHOT   (WHAT SHE SEES)
As Monte goes to his car, one of the parking attendants holds the door open for him. Monte hands him a tip—the check that Mildred just gave him. The attendant reacts as Monte drives away.

232.   SIDE ANGLE   MILDRED
as she puts her head down on her arms.

                                           DISSOLVE TO:

233.   PAN SHOT   INT. HAWAIIAN CAFE
to show dance band on stand and singer hard at work. The CAMERA PANS past dancers on the floor to a booth at one side, which contains Ted Forrester and Veda. Ted is mooning at Veda.

234.   MED. CLOSE   TED AND VEDA   (IN BOOTH)
Ted is a clean-cut, very earnest young man whose idealistic nature is hardly a match for Veda's predatory instincts.

TED:
    You do love me, don't you, Veda?

VEDA (watching the dancers):
    Madly.

TED (aggrieved):
    Well, you don't say it like you do.

VEDA (with a trace of irritation):
    Oh, don't be tiresome, Ted . . . please. I can't *bear* it when you make noises like a wounded cow.

TED:
    I'm sorry. I can't help it. I can't sleep nights thinking about you.

VEDA (a perfunctory pat on the cheek):
>You're sweet. And I do love you, really I do.

Ted beams dizzily as Veda looks up.[68]

WALLY'S VOICE (off-scene):
>Well—well—this looks serious.

235. FULL SHOT   BOOTH
as Ted looks happily from Wally to Veda.

TED:
>It is.

VEDA:
>Yes. We finally made up our minds, Wally.

WALLY (snaps his fingers at a waiter and then starts to sit down):
>This calls for a celebration . . . (To Ted.) Shove over, Romeo.

236. TWO SHOT   TED AND WALLY
As Wally sits beside him, Ted looks at him gratefully.

TED:
>You've been swell to us, Mr. Fay.

WALLY:
>Forget it, son. I like doing things for other people. Don't I, Veda?

237. GROUP SHOT   THE THREE
as Veda and Wally smile at each other in perfect communion.

VEDA:
>Oh, absolutely.

A waiter arrives with some champagne in a bucket. The glasses are tucked under his arm.

WALLY:
>   Here we are . . . (He looks annoyed by the glasses,
>   takes them from waiter, who shrugs and goes away.)
>   You'd think we never served champagne in my
>   place . . .

Wally is struggling with the cork.

238.   FULL SHOT   BOOTH (INCLUDING PEOPLE AT A NEARBY
TABLE)
as Wally finally pops the cork, making a noise like a pistol
shot. The people nearby jump nervously, then turn and
stare.

239.   THREE SHOT   BOOTH

WALLY (genially):
>   No cause for alarm . . . (Indicates the bottle, then
>   pours.) Here, you kids, try this on for size.

Wally fills his own glass, then lifts it.

WALLY:
>   To . . . true love.

They drink Over his glass Wally winks his off eye at
Veda. Veda's eyes shift to Ted.[69]

DISSOLVE TO:

240.   INT. MILDRED'S OFFICE
CAMERA PANS with Mildred as she stalks back and forth,
then PANS AWAY from her to Mr. Jones, the accountant, a
harmless little man who is sitting at the desk, patiently
waiting for Mildred's attention. He coughs discreetly.

MR. JONES:
>   About the Laguna Beach statement, Mrs. Pierce.

241.   CLOSE   ON MILDRED
as she suddenly re-collects herself.

MILDRED:
I'm sorry. I was thinking about something else. What about the Laguna Beach statement?

242. MED. CLOSE SHOT   JONES
as he consults his books and adjusts his spectacles.

MR. JONES (pedantically):
The receipts of the establishment at Laguna Beach have dropped roughly seven percent during the last month . . . nearly eight percent. (Shakes his head sadly.) Tsk, tsk.

243. FULL SHOT   OFFICE
as Ida comes in. Mildred looks at her.

IDA:
A Mrs. Forrester to see you. I told her to wait on the patio. (She indicates.)

MILDRED:
She wants to see me? What about?

IDA:
Veda.

Mildred goes toward the patio. The accountant looks at Ida with great annoyance and contempt.

MR. JONES (to Ida):
You always interrupt!

IDA (wolfishly):
It's because I want to be alone with you . . . Come here and let me bite you, you darling boy.

Mr. Jones shrinks away, a little frightened at the prospect.

244. EXT. RESTAURANT   PATIO
as a tall, distinguished-looking lady rises to meet Mildred. This is Mrs. Forrester, Ted's mother. Mrs. Forrester is glacially elegant and poised.

MRS. FORRESTER:
Mrs. Pierce? (Mildred nods.) I'm Mrs. Forrester. Ted's mother.

MILDRED:
I'm very glad to know you.

MRS. FORRESTER:
And I've been looking forward *so* much to meeting *you*, Mrs. Pierce. I'm *sure* we're going to work out our little problem spendidly.

MILDRED (surprised):
What little problem?

MRS. FORRESTER:
Veda hasn't told you?

MILDRED:
Told me what?

MRS. FORRESTER:
Veda has somehow got the idea that—well, I *understand it*, of course. Any girl wants to get married. But Ted had no such thing in mind. I want that made clear.

MILDRED:
You mean—they're engaged? Veda and your son?

MRS. FORRESTER (her voice is becoming a little high and strident):
Yes . . . but I'm *quite* sure you'll agree with me, Mrs. Pierce, that *any* discussion of marriage between them would be *most* undesirable.

MILDRED (sharply and suspiciously):
Why should Veda want to marry your son, if he doesn't want to marry her?

MRS. FORRESTER (angrily):
I'm not a mind reader, Mrs. Pierce. But let me tell you one thing. If you, or that girl, or anybody employs any more tricks, trying to blackmail my boy into—

MILDRED (exploding):
> Trying to *what?*

MRS. FORRESTER (completely losing her temper):
> Understand me, Mrs. Pierce, I shall prevent this
> marriage. I shall prevent it in any way that I can!

MILDRED:
> I don't think you need worry, Mrs. Forrester . . .
> Having you in my family is a rather dismal prospect.
> I'll talk to Veda.

Mildred turns her back as, mottled with rage, Mrs. Forrester leaves. Mildred is looking extremely thoughtful.

> DISSOLVE TO:

245.   EXT. GLENDALE HOUSE
as Mildred arrives and goes up the walk looking very
businesslike and purposeful.

246.   INT. LIVING ROOM   GLENDALE HOUSE
where Veda is talking to Wally, who is reclining at ease
behind his desk. Veda is standing.

WALLY (to Veda):
> The next move is up to them. When we got out that
> warrant for his arrest, we showed that we meant
> business . . .

As she hears the SOUND of the door closing, Veda cuts him
off with an abrupt cautioning wave of the hand. Veda
selects a cigarette from her silver case, as Mildred enters.

MILDRED:
> I want to talk to you.

VEDA:
> What about?

MILDRED (meaningly):
> Mrs. Forrester was in to see me today.

VEDA:
> Oh?

She exchanges a look with Wally.

MILDRED (directly to Wally):
This is private, Wally.

VEDA (calmly):
He knows about it.

MILDRED (amazed):
He knows that you and Ted want to get married?

VEDA:
Want to get married?

247. CLOSE ON MILDRED

VEDA'S VOICE (OVER):
We *are* married. We were married on my birthday.

248. GROUP SHOT   MILDRED, VEDA, AND WALLY

VEDA (continuing):
I'm sorry, but it's done.

WALLY (smoothly):
You see, Mildred, Veda has been trying to spare you.
She wanted to make things easy for you, and she
asked me to help.

MILDRED (still looking at Veda in stunned amazement):
Veda, why didn't you tell me?

VEDA:
I wanted to . . . so many times . . . but you seemed so
far away. I couldn't somehow. I was afraid.

Mildred melts completely.

MILDRED:
Afraid? Of your own mother?

There are tears in Mildred's eyes as Veda comes to her.

VEDA:
> Mother—I've been so miserable. I made a mistake—
> and I didn't know how to tell you . . .

MILDRED:
> Don't you love this boy?

Veda shakes her head.

MILDRED:
> I'm sorry for that—but maybe we don't belong in such
> a family anyhow.

WALLY (quickly striking while the iron is hot):
> That's right. Veda doesn't love this kid. She made a
> mistake. The only thing we can do is settle the case out
> of court. It's the only clean, quick way of handling the
> situation.

VEDA:
> Wally is right, Mother.

For an instant Mildred is indecisive, then, softened by the
realization of her daughter's situation, she gives in completely.

MILDRED:
> All right, Wally. Do what you think best.

Again she puts her arms around Veda and holds her
tenderly.

> DISSOLVE TO:

249. INT. FORRESTER LIBRARY
At the desk is Williams, attorney for the Forresters. Facing
him is a group consisting of Wally, Veda, Bert, and
Mildred. Sitting behind Williams is Mrs. Forrester and her
son Ted, who looks sheepish.

WILLIAMS (reading from a legal document):
> ". . . and I hereby, of my own free will, renounce all
> right and title that I or my heirs and assignees may
> have to any monies or estate, real or otherwise, which

195

will accrue or evolve to Theodore Ellison Forrester, in exchange for considerations of value received."

He looks up, taking off his thick, horn-rimmed spectacles.

WILLIAMS (to Ted and his mother):
Are you agreeable to this waiver?

Mrs. Forrester nods, grim lipped. Ted doesn't look very happy.

TED (timidly):
Please—why can't we stay married? I don't see why we—

Mrs. Forrester nudges him heavily.

MRS. FORRESTER:
Theodore . . . you will be so good as to keep quiet.

TED (subsiding miserably):
Yes, Mother.

WILLIAMS (to Wally and Veda):
I think we may assume that the waiver is acceptable. Will you sign here, please?

Veda makes a move. Wally restrains her.

WALLY (perfectly at ease):
Sure. Glad to.[70] There's one little formality we should discuss first, however.

WILLIAMS:
What's that, Mr. Fay?

WALLY:
The financial settlement, Mr. Williams. My client would like ten thousand dollars.

Mr. Williams looks at Mrs. Forrester and gets his cue from her frown.

WILLIAMS:
I think I'm safe in observing that almost anyone would like ten thousand dollars, Mr. Fay. But—

WALLY:
But—?

WILLIAMS (smiling):
We see no necessity for a financial settlement of any kind.

WALLY (also smiling):
Don't you?

WILLIAMS (very pleasant):
No.

WALLY (also pleasant):
You will.

WILLIAMS:
I doubt it.

MILDRED (breaking in):
I don't understand all this . . . as far as I know, there's no need of a financial settlement. All we're interested in is . . .

VEDA (desperately):
Please, Mother! I need the money. I'm going to have a baby.

WILLIAMS, MRS. FORRESTER, AND TED (in that order):
What?

MILDRED:
Veda—

Wally is smiling benignly on all concerned, particularly Mr. Williams.

WALLY:
So you see . . . ten thousand dollars is not unreasonable.

197

WILLIAMS (his pleasant manner gone):
This is moral backmail, sir?[71]

MRS. FORRESTER:
I won't pay it!

WALLY:
Yes, you will, Mrs. Forrester. Ask your attorney.

Mrs. Forrester looks at Williams. He nods. She taps Ted and motions him out of the room, following him herself.

WALLY (to Williams):
Yes?

WILLIAMS:
Yes.

WALLY:
You can mail the check.[72]

Wally takes the agreement drawn up, borrows Mr. Williams's desk pen and signs it, then tries to pocket the pen. Mr. Williams calls his attention to the fact that it isn't his, and Wally gives it back. Mildred is comforting Veda.

DISSOLVE TO:

250. CLOSE SHOT   CHECK IN VEDA'S HAND
It is a cashier's check made out to Veda Pierce Forrester and is drawn on the Beverly Hills Guarantee and Trust Co., for ten thousand dollars. The CAMERA PANS UP to Veda's face as she kisses the check.

VEDA (smiling to herself):
Well, that's that.

251. FULL SHOT   LIVING ROOM   GLENDALE HOUSE
Mildred is taking off her hat and removing her gloves at the piano.

MILDRED:
I'm sorry about that boy. He seemed very nice.

VEDA (carelessly):
Oh, Ted's all right, really. (She laughs softly.) Did you see the look on his face when we told him he was going to be a father?

MILDRED:
I wish you wouldn't joke about it, Veda.

Suddenly Veda throws her head back and laughs harshly and metallically, then she stops abruptly.

VEDA:
Mother, you're a scream. Really you are. The next thing I know you'll be knitting little garments.

MILDRED (hurt):
Why not?

VEDA (levelly):
If I were you, I'd save myself the trouble.

MILDRED:
Now don't be silly, Veda . . .

Suddenly she stops talking and stares at Veda with growing horror in her face. Veda stares back, her eyes stony and a half-smile on her face. Mildred wets her lips before she speaks.

MILDRED:
You're not going to have a baby.

VEDA (shrugging):
At this stage it's a matter of opinion. And in my opinion I'm going to have a baby. I can always be mistaken.

MILDRED (horrified; her voice shaking):
How could you do such a thing?

VEDA (a silent shrug):
I got the money, didn't I? I'll have to give Wally part of it to keep him quiet, but there's enough left for me.

MILDRED:
> Money—that's what you live for, isn't it? You'll do
> anything for money—even blackmail.

VEDA (coldly):
> Oh, grow up.

MILDRED (disregarding her):
> I've never denied you anything . . . anything that
> money could buy I've given you. And it wasn't
> enough. All right, Veda . . . things are going to be
> different now. You're going to give that check
> back . . .

Veda calmly shakes her head, completely at ease.

VEDA:
> No. I'm not going to give back the check. (Sav-
> agely.) Why do you think I went to the trouble of
> getting it? Why do you think I want money so
> badly?

MILDRED:
> Why?

Veda looks at her mother levelly and then slowly
chooses a cigarette for herself.

VEDA (with calm deliberation):
> Are you sure you want to know?

Mildred nods as Veda lights her cigarette.

VEDA (with mounting intensity):
> Then I'll tell you. With enough money I can get
> away from you . . . from you and your chickens
> and your pies and your kitchens and everything
> that smells of grease. I can get away from this shack
> with its cheap furniture, and away from this town
> and its dollar days, and its furniture factories, and
> its women that wear uniforms and its men that
> wear overalls. With money I can get away from

every rotten, stinking thing that even reminds me
of this place—or you.[73]

MILDRED (quietly):
Veda—I think I'm seeing you as you are for the first
time in my life. You're cheap and horrible.

VEDA (with venomous hatred):
You think now you've made a little money you can
get a new hairdo and some expensive clothes and
turn yourself into a lady, but you can't, because
you'll never be anything but a common frump,
whose father lived over a grocery store and whose
mother took in washing. It makes me shrivel up to
think you ever carried me.

Mildred has been perfectly still throughout this tirade.
Now, with great deliberation, she walks forward a few
steps and slaps Veda across the face. Veda strikes her
back heavily. Disregarding Veda's kicking, biting fury,
Mildred tears the check out of Veda's hands and then
backs away tearing the check into shreds, with Veda
clawing at her in a desperate effort to get it back.

They stand facing each other, both breathing hard.
Veda is horrified by what her mother has done.

MILDRED (a low, hoarse voice):
Get out, Veda. Get your things out of this house
right now or I'll throw them into the
street . . . and you with them. Get out before I kill
you.

Veda hesitates and then realizes that this time it's different from all other times. She turns on her heel and
flounces out. Mildred stands perfectly still, her face set
in fury.

FADE OUT

FADE IN

252.   FULL SHOT   EXT. BEVERLY HILLS RESTAURANT
SHOOTING TOWARD parking lot, which is empty. A car

drives up and stops. In the background a gardener is working, the only sign of life.

MILDRED'S VOICE (OVER SCENE):
I went away for a while. I traveled. But not far enough. Something kept pulling me back . . . and finally I gave in. I went home.

Mildred gets out of the car, and starts toward the restaurant. The CAMERA PANS to the door, where Lottie is polishing the brasswork.

MILDRED:
Good morning, Lottie.

Lottie looks up, her face lighting up with pleasure.

LOTTIE:
Why, Miz Pierce! Oh my—this is a day for rejoicing, it certainly is. You've been away *so* long.

MILDRED (smiling at the welcome):
I've been to Mexico.

LOTTIE (enchanted):
Is that a fact? It's sure nice to have you back. (She opens the door for Mildred.)

MILDRED:
Thank you, Lottie. (Pausing.) I'm very glad to see you.

LOTTIE:
Likewise, Mrs. Pierce. This is a *happy* day.

Mildred goes in.

253.   PAN SHOT   MILDRED
as she crosses the busy interior of the restaurant and goes toward the office door and enters. The door is marked Manager.

254.   INT. OFFICE
with Ida sitting at the desk, working over menus. She
gets up as Mildred enters.

IDA:
   Well—well . . . long time no see. How was Mexico?

MILDRED:
   Nice. How is business?

IDA:
   Wonderful. (Indicating.) Want your desk back?

MILDRED:
   No, thanks. On you it looks good.

The two women smile at each other. Mildred takes out a
cigarette and lights it. Her hand trembles. Ida notices,
and Mildred sees that she does.

MILDRED (grimly):
   Nothing like a good long rest, is there? Got a drink
   handy?

Ida goes to a cellarette and pours a drink and a water
chaser.

IDA:
   You never used to drink during the day.

MILDRED:
   I never used to drink at all. Here's to those who
   taught me how.[74] (Toasting.) Men!

She tosses off the drink. Ida watches her.

IDA:
   That's the way it is, Mildred. It's a man's world. If
   you succeed, if you show signs of getting up in the
   world . . . then the knives come out. I never yet
   met a man who didn't have the instincts of a heel.

(A pause and then she shrugs.) I sometimes wish I could get along without 'em.

MILDRED:
You've never been married, have you, Ida?

IDA:
When men are around me they suddenly get allergic to wedding rings. (A rueful grimace.) I'm the big sister type. You know—good old Ida . . . you can talk with her man to man. (Reflective.) I'm getting very tired of men talking man to man with me. Think I'll have a drink myself.

She takes Mildred's glass and goes and pours two more drinks.

MILDRED (a strained attempt at being casual):
Er—see anybody I know lately?

IDA (calmly):
You mean Veda. I wondered how long it'd take you to get around to that.

MILDRED:
Yes. I mean Veda. (Eagerly.) Have you seen her, Ida? Is she all right?

IDA (crossing with drinks):
Why don't you forget her?

MILDRED (miserable):
I can't. I've tried, but I can't.

IDA:
Well—try, try again. That's my motto!

She drinks her drink.

MILDRED (staring into space):
You don't know how it is, Ida. Being a mother. She's a part of me. Maybe she didn't turn out as well as I hoped she would when she was born . . .

but she's my daughter. I can't forget that. I went away to try. I was all mixed up. I didn't know where I was or what I wanted. Now I know. Now I'm sure of one thing at least. I want my daughter back.

IDA (shrugs):
Personally, Veda has convinced me that alligators have the right idea. (She drinks, then explains.) They eat their young.

The phone rings. Ida picks it up.

IDA:
Yes? Who's calling? Who? Hang on. (To Mildred.) It's Bert. How'd he know you were back?

MILDRED:
I left a message for him to call me here. (She takes the phone.) Hello, Bert. I know you're busy . . . but I want to talk to you. Do you know where Veda is? (A pause.) *Why* won't you tell me . . . ? All right. Eight o'clock. I'll be ready. (She hangs up.)

IDA:
He won't tell you where she is?

MILDRED:
He wants to have dinner with me tonight, and tell me then.

IDA:
Oh. How is he?[75]

MILDRED (abstracted):
What—Oh, he's fine. He's working now.

IDA:
You're kidding.

MILDRED:
No. He's got a job at Condor Aircraft.

IDA:
>Hmmm. The manpower shortage must be worse than we think.

>>>DISSOLVE TO:

255. ANGLE SHOT   HAWAIIAN CAFE   MILDRED AND BERT
in one of the booths. The CAMERA MOVES IN on them. In the background a mixed crowd is dancing to the music of a rather tired orchestra. We HEAR but do not see a vocalist singing with the band. She is just finishing the number.

MILDRED (to Bert; with distaste):
>I never did like this place. And I don't see why you insisted on coming down here for dinner.

BERT (a nervous manner):
>I'm sorry I did now. I thought it was a good idea at the time, but now I'm not so sure.

MILDRED:
>I don't understand you, Bert. And I don't think you're being very kind. You promised to take me to Veda . . .

BERT (completely miserable):
>I have, Mildred. (Without looking, he nods his head slightly.)

With a puzzled frown, Mildred looks in the direction he indicated. Then her face stiffens with shock at what she sees.[76]

256. DANCE STAND   (FROM THEIR ANGLE)
The vocalist we have been hearing in the background is Veda. She finishes her number and takes her bows. She is dressed in an extreme evening gown and looks much older than her years. Her manner is assured and deliberately provocative. She smiles at a sailor dancing, who whistles up at her. The sailor's partner drags him away. Veda starts off the stage.

257. CLOSE ON MILDRED

BERT'S VOICE:
 I'm sorry I did it like this, Mildred . . . but I didn't
 know how to tell you.

Mildred gets to her feet and starts in the direction taken
by Veda.

258. TWO SHOT   MILDRED AND BERT
 as Bert also rises.

BERT:
 Take it easy, Mildred. You can't do anything . . . Mildred!

Mildred doesn't even hear him. She goes away. Bert sits
down and tosses off his drink savagely.

258A. AT PASSAGEWAY   LEADING TO DRESSING ROOMS
 as a waiter gestures down the hall, evidently in answer
 to a question from Mildred. She starts down the hall.
 Wally comes into scene and stops her.

258B. TWO SHOT   WALLY AND MILDRED
 Wally catches Mildred by the arm.

WALLY:
 Hey—you been away so long you've forgotten your
 business partner?

MILDRED:
 Hello, Wally. (She tries to disengage her arm.)

WALLY (blocking her off from the passage):
 What's on your mind? You here to see me?

MILDRED:
 I'm going to take Veda home.

WALLY:
 Yeah— Does she know that?

MILDRED:
> No. I wish you'd help me, Wally.

WALLY:
> Not me. She's your daughter. (Mildred starts by
> him. He restrains her with a light touch.) I've never
> been a father— (he knocks on the nearest wood) but
> Veda has been working here for a month now, and I
> think I know how to handle her. Let me give you
> some advice. If you want her to do anything . . .
> knock her down first.

Mildred goes on down the passage. He shrugs and
walks away.

259. INT. DRESSING ROOM (ANGLE SHOT AT MIRROR)
where Miriam Ellis, a flashy blonde, is touching up her
makeup. Veda is just finishing putting on a fresh pair of
stockings.

MIRIAM (looking at herself in mirror, critically):
> Maybe he's right—

VEDA (not paying much attention):
> Who?

MIRIAM:
> Wally. He says I look like who done it and ran
> away!

VEDA:
> How is your big romance with Wally getting on?

MIRIAM (shrugs):
> You know Wally. He proposed to me last night . . .
> (Dabs at her lips, surveys the result, then con-
> tinues.) You know what he had the nerve to say to
> me? He says to me, "Hey, you, let's get married or
> somethin'!"

VEDA:
> What did you say?

MIRIAM:
Let's get married or nothin', that's what I said.

VEDA (with a bored air):
Then what did he say?

MIRIAM:
I'm tellin' you—what could he say? I mean he was floored. "Are you kiddin'," he says. "No," I says, "and what's more . . ."

Seen through the mirror, the door opens. Mildred enters.

MIRIAM (to Mildred, by way of the mirror):
You got the wrong place, lady. You want . . . (She gestures.)

After one swift look at her mother, Veda goes right on with her stockings.

VEDA (to Miriam, with complete disinterest):
It's all right, Miriam—she's my mother.

MIRIAM:
Oh. No kidding! I didn't know you had a mother.

VEDA:
Everybody has a mother.

Veda goes to a wardrobe for a smock, ignoring Mildred.

MIRIAM (abstracted; she's curious about what gives here):
Oh sure—I guess you're right.

VEDA (to Mildred):
This is Miriam Ellis, Mother— She sings.

MIRIAM (modestly):
That's what they tell me anyhow, Mrs. Pierce.

VEDA (seeing that this could go on interminably):
What can I do for you, Mother?

MILDRED (hesitantly):
I'd— I'd like to speak to you.

Putting on the smock, Veda goes back and sits down and starts going over her makeup.

VEDA:
Go ahead.

MILDRED (looking at Miriam and back to Veda):
I—uh—that is . . .

VEDA (to Miriam, calmly):
Why don't you go see if Wally wants you?

MIRIAM (shaking her head):
He won't. (Then it dawns.) Oh—pardon me, I'm sure.

Miriam gets up and hurries out, giving Mildred a final curious glance. Mildred just stares at Veda.

VEDA (into the mirror):
Well?

MILDRED (putting her hands on Veda's shoulders):
Veda, I want you to come home . . .

Veda avoids Mildred's touch.

MILDRED (continuing):
. . . you don't belong here. This isn't your kind of life.

VEDA:
No? What *is* my kind of life, Mother?

Veda goes back to her makeup job, again cool and assured.

MILDRED:
I don't know . . . whatever makes you happy, I guess. That's all I want for you, Veda. Everything I've ever done was to make you happy.

VEDA:
Do you think I was happy in Glendale, Mother?

MILDRED (meaningly):
Are you happy *here*, Veda?

VEDA (shrugs):
When I first came here I used to cry occasionally.
But I've gotten over that.

MILDRED (bitterly):
I haven't.

VEDA (impatiently):
I'm sorry, Mother. I know I've made you unhappy,
but— (She shrugs.)

MILDRED:
It isn't easy for me to beg like this, Veda . . . but I
want you to come home.

This angers Veda. She turns savagely.

VEDA:
No, Mother! You must think I'm on a string. Go
away, Veda! Come back, Veda! (She shakes her
head.) It isn't that easy. (She gets up and takes off
her smock.) I'm free now. No one tells me what to
do and what not to do. I do what I think best. And I
like it that way.

MILDRED (a pathetic attempt at brightness):
I've had the house redecorated. And all new furniture. Even a new piano, Veda. You'd like it, I know.

VEDA (not unkindly):
You still don't understand, do you? You think new
curtains are enough to make me happy. (She goes
to Mildred.)

260.   TWO SHOT   VEDA AND MILDRED
VEDA:
No. I want more than that . . . I want the kind of

life that Monte taught me. And you won't give it to me. (She puts her arms around Mildred, and in a softer tone continues.) [77] I'm sorry for all the trouble I caused. But if I went home . . . it would start all over again. You know that. You know how I am. The way you want to live isn't good enough for me.

MILDRED:
If I lived in a wonderful house, in a beautiful district and knew all the right people, you'd be willing enough to come back.

VEDA (a slight shrug):
But you don't, do you, Mother?

The door opens and Miriam comes back in. Veda disregards her to primp her hair in the mirror.

MIRIAM (to Mildred):
Sorry to interrupt . . . but you can powder your nose just so long, then people begin to look at you funny. (To Veda.) Anyhow, your number is coming up.

VEDA:
All right. (She starts for the door.) Good-bye, Mother.

MILDRED:
Wait—when can I see you again?

VEDA (at door):
Any time, Mother. Just come in the front door . . . and buy yourself a beer.

She goes out. Miriam is shocked by Veda's attitude.

MIRIAM:
What a thing to say to her mudder . . . Why, I'd smack her face!

MILDRED:
No. I've got a better idea.

The CAMERA HOLDS on Mildred. She is smiling a little.

DISSOLVE TO:

261. EXT. PASADENA HOUSE   DAY
showing in detail its rather antique appearance. The
lines of the house are basically good, but the obsession
for rococo gew-gaws and facades of thirty years ago
make the building rather repulsive. An iron deer is
nibbling at the lawn, for instance. A car (Mildred's) is
pulled up before the entrance, beside a large For Sale
sign.

DISSOLVE TO:

262. INT. PASADENA HOUSE   (DAY SHOT, BUT GLOOMY)
The interior is very much like the exterior, except that
it's more dusty and less well lighted. Monte and
Mildred are just coming down from upstairs.

MONTE:
    Look—you can't be seriously thinking of buying
    this place.

MILDRED:
    You're some salesman.

MONTE (he laughs self-consciously):
    Well then—so much for upstairs. Pretty gloomy,
    isn't it? Not quite so bad down here.

They enter the sitting room, off the reception hall.

263. INT. SITTING ROOM
still with that dusty look, but somewhat less forbidding.

MONTE:
    This used to be the sitting room. Still is. I do all my
    sitting here. Drink?

MILDRED:
    Thanks.

Mildred looks about the room with a cold interest, as
Monte mixes drinks. On a marble-topped table, there is

a portable gas burner, together with a box of eggs, a half-loaf of bread, a half-filled bottle of milk, and a plate with the remnants of an egg on it. Mildred shakes her head a little and looks at Monte. He smiles a trifle grimly.

MONTE:
The pride of the Beragons, as you see, is not exactly rolling in wealth. Say when. (He pours.) [78]

MILDRED:
When. What happened to your orange groves?

MONTE (a bit rueful):
Sold for taxes. Like everything else.

MILDRED:
The beach house, too? That was beautiful.

MONTE:
No, not the beach house. I have an uncle with a little money. He won't let me sell the beach house. (He grins.) He's hoping to foreclose on it instead.

MILDRED:
Mmmmmm—sounds like a nice uncle.

Monte crosses with the drinks and gives one to Mildred, then sits down, perfectly at ease.

MONTE:
Now—what do you want, Mildred?

MILDRED:
I don't understand.

MONTE:
Yes, you do. You don't really want to buy this— (gesturing) this antiquated tomb. You'd be out of your mind.

MILDRED:
Oh, I don't know. It's not such a bad house . . . . A

little remodeling would do wonders . . . Take off some of the gingerbread and redecorate inside, and—

Monte is smiling at her, patiently waiting for her to get through. She stops, lamely.

MILDRED (wryly):
   My businesslike air isn't fooling you much, is it?

MONTE (quietly):
   No. I remember too well, Mildred. I remember how it was with us once. And so do you. It isn't something either of us can forget.

MILDRED (seeing an opening):
   Monte—you haven't forgotten?

MONTE (to his drink):
   Not for an hour . . . (He shakes his head and then drinks.) Even this— (indicating glass) doesn't help.

MILDRED (softly):
   Then—you can do me a great kindness, Monte . . .

MONTE:
   If I can.

MILDRED:
   Ask me to marry you.

For an instant there is silence as Monte looks at Mildred. Then he sets his glass down carefully.

MONTE:
   Why?

MILDRED (dryly):
   Your attitude isn't exactly enthusiastic.

MONTE:
   You went to considerable trouble to get rid of me once. Naturally I'm a little startled by your proposal of marriage— (A smile.) This is so sudden, Mildred.

MILDRED:

I have my own personal reason for wanting to marry you.

MONTE:

A reason named Veda, I think.

MILDRED:

Why should it be?

MONTE:

The reason for anything you do is usually Veda.

MILDRED:

Whether it is or not, what's your answer?

MONTE:

I can't afford you, Mildred. You've got money. I haven't. All I've got left is pride and a name . . . and I can't sell either.

MILDRED:

Why not?

MONTE (bitterly):

I'm not enjoying this, Mildred. It's different now, from the way it was that day at the beach house . . .

MILDRED:

I haven't forgotten, Monte.

MONTE (going to her):

Neither have I. I want you to love me again as you did then . . . I need that more than anything else. I'm lost without it. I told you that day I know you were the only woman in the world for me. I loved you then, Mildred . . . and I love you now.

MILDRED:

Then why—

MONTE (turning away):

I can't marry you, Mildred. I won't take tips from

you the way I used to. (A pause.) Of course, if I
owned a share in your business— (He stops.)

MILDRED (slowly):
I see. I think I understand. (Ironic.) How much of a
share does your pride require, Monte?

MONTE (going to her again):
Don't put it like that, Mildred. You know it hurts
me to do this . . . I'm doing it only because I have
to—

MILDRED (steadily):
How much of a share?

MONTE (after a pause):
One third.

MILDRED:
All right. (He tries to kiss her. She turns away.)
Sold. One Beragon.

DISSOLVE TO:

264.   INSERT   SOCIETY COLUMN
with a two-column head consisting of an informal por-
trait of Mildred and Monte at their wedding ceremony.
Monte is helping Mildred cut the cake. Underneath is
the first caption:
Businesswoman and Beragon Heir Wed

followed by the story:
One of Pasadena's most popular young
men about town today married Mildred
Pierce, well-known owner of the chain
of restaurants that bear her name. Etc.

MILDRED'S VOICE (COMING OVER):
Monte and I were married six months ago . . . just
before Christmas . . .[79]

DISSOLVE TO:

265. FULL SHOT FOYER
as Lottie crosses to the front door and opens it. Bert is standing there. Lottie takes his hat.

LOTTIE:
Mr. Pierce—my, it's nice to see you.

BERT:
You too, Lottie. Is Mrs. Pierce—Mrs. Beragon—is she home?

LOTTIE (gesturing with a thumb):
In there. (Then remembering her new dignity.) I mean—this way, please.

She ushers him toward the living room.

265A. FULL SHOT LIVING ROOM
as Lottie and Bert appear at the door.

LOTTIE (loudly):
Mr. Albert Pierce. (Then she breaks up and giggles and goes away.)

Mildred crosses to meet Bert.

MILDRED (ruefully):
Poor Lottie is a little overwhelmed by it all . . . It's good to see you, Bert.

BERT:
You too. Just thought I'd drive by and say hello. Hope you don't mind?

MILDRED:
Of course not.

They sit on the davenport. Mildred offers him a cigarette from a box on the table.

MILDRED:
You didn't come to the wedding.[80]

BERT:
I read about it.

MILDRED (chattering):
We didn't have any time for a honeymoon. Monte's folks, I mean—family, were the only people at the wedding. There was a sort of reception afterwards. I met a lot of his friends—

BERT (suddenly interrupting):
Mildred! I know I've got a lot of nerve to ask you this— (he pauses; she listens nervously) but—do you really love this guy?

MILDRED (defiantly):
I married him, didn't I?

BERT:
That doesn't answer my question.

MILDRED (more calmly):
Monte's okay.

BERT (quietly):
That still doesn't answer me. Are you in love with this guy?

MILDRED (turning away):
No, I don't exactly love him . . .

Bert's face glows a little, but he instantly hides it.

MILDRED:
. . . but we understand each other. And then, I thought—maybe if I moved away from the other house, and fixed this place up—I thought maybe—

BERT:
Veda would come back?

Mildred is on the defensive for a second, remembering the old quarrels. Then she resigns herself to it and nods.

BERT:
I thought that was why.

MILDRED (almost pleading):
I know you think I'm a fool, Bert, but I can't help it. I'll do anything—anything—to get her back. I couldn't leave her where she was—could I, Bert?

BERT (rising; decidedly):
No, I guess not. Anyhow, that's all I wanted to know.

MILDRED (also rising):
We'll always fight about her, won't we?

Bert's eyes are kind as he turns her around so that she faces the window.

BERT (smiles gently):
I brought you a wedding present. Look out the window.

Mildred looks a little bewildered, then crosses to the window and looks out.

266.   DRIVE IN FRONT OF HOUSE   (AS SEEN THROUGH WINDOW)
Veda is getting out of her coupe, which is standing there.

267.   MILDRED AND BERT
Mildred gasps, turns to Bert in astonishment.

MILDRED:
Bert! Did you ask her to come with you?

BERT:
No, she called me up. She tried to pretend it was for something else but I got the truth out of her. She wanted to come home, Mildred.

MILDRED (controlling her emotion with difficulty):
Tell her to come in.

Bert leaves Mildred. She walks slowly away from the window, twisting and untwisting her hands. She reaches the mantelpiece and leans against it, holding herself in check.

268.   FULL SHOT FRONT DOOR (SHOOTING PAST MILDRED)
as Bert opens it and reveals Veda standing on the threshold.

269.   CLOSE ON MILDRED
as she sees her daughter.

    MILDRED (almost inaudible):
      Veda . . .

270.   CLOSE ON VEDA
as she smiles tremulously.

    VEDA:
      Mother . . .

271.   FULL SHOT VEDA, MILDRED, BERT
as Mildred and Veda go to each other.

272.   TWO SHOT MILDRED AND VEDA
Mildred and Veda embrace, smiling at each other happily.

    VEDA:
      Oh, Mother . . . I wanted to come weeks ago . . . and when Christmas came I couldn't stay away—

    MILDRED:
      I'm glad, darling . . .

273.   FULL SHOT (INCLUDING BERT)
who is beginning to feel like a fifth wheel. He smiles, starts to say something, and gets disregarded.

    VEDA (to Mildred):
      I'll change, Mother. I promise. I'll never say mean things to you again . . .

MILDRED:
> I said mean things too . . . Oh, Veda . . .

Again they embrace, oblivious of Bert, who fumbles around a little and then walks out, closing the door behind him. Veda and Mildred break apart at the SOUND of the door closing.

MILDRED (calling):
> Bert! (To Veda.) I forgot to thank him . . .

Mildred goes to the door and runs after Bert.[81]

274.   MED. CLOSE ON VEDA
as left alone, she takes out a cigarette. A hand comes into the SHOT, offering a light. CAMERA PULLS BACK to reveal Monte, standing there and smiling.

MONTE:
> Well, well . . . the prodigal returneth. I'll arrange to have a fatted calf for dinner . . .

Veda takes the light he offers, with a sidelong glance at him.

275.   WIDER ANGLE (AS MILDRED COMES BACK)
into the house. She smiles at Monte and Veda.

MILDRED:
> Monte—Veda's come home! She's going to stay with us!

VEDA (looking at Monte):
> That is—if Monte doesn't mind.

MONTE (smiling a little):
> I think it's wonderful. Just don't call me Father.

DISSOLVE TO:

FADE IN

276.   CLOSE ON BIRTHDAY CAKE
with nineteen candles and the inscription Happy Birth-

day to Veda. We hear the muffled SOUNDS of the people standing around, giggles, comments, etc.

The CAMERA PULLS BACK to reveal Veda standing by the cake, as she puffs out her cheeks and blows out the candles. There is an uproar of congratulations, and Veda starts to cut the cake.

276A. MED. CLOSE (AT SIDEBOARD) (PARTY IN BACKGROUND) where Lottie is in executive control of the caterer's maids and butlers. Lottie is handing another maid several bottles of champagne from the sideboard.

LOTTIE:
Eloise, watch out how you pour that champagne. It's Veuve Cliquot 1927.

ELOISE:
Is that better than '28?

LOTTIE:
Definitely.[82]

Lottie starts for living room, carrying a tray of canapes. The CAMERA TRUCKS AND PANS with her. A phone in a recess begins to RING.

LOTTIE (answering the phone):
Beragon residence . . . who shall I say is calling? Oh, yes'm . . . yes, Miss Mildred.

She sets the phone down on the telephone table and goes off. The CAMERA MOVES IN on the phone.

276B. MED. CLOSE ON MILDRED INT. BUSINESS OFFICE who is lighting a cigarette as she waits for someone to answer. Her office is half-filled with smoke. We hear the SOUND of conversation in the background. Mildred looks in that direction.

JONES'S VOICE:
. . . but it's not right, on such short notice—

LAWYER'S VOICE:
>Business is business, Mr. Jones. Business is business.

MILDRED (into phone):
>Hello, Ida? This is Mildred. How is the party going?

276C. CLOSE ON IDA (AT THE PHONE)

IDA:
>Veda just cut the cake . . .

276D. CLOSE ON MILDRED (AT THE PHONE)

MILDRED:
>She didn't wait for me?

IDA'S VOICE (over phone):
>She said you wouldn't mind . . .

MILDRED (wryly):
>Well, I do . . . a little.

LAWYER'S VOICE:
>Out of the question! Absolutely out of the question!

MILDRED (with a glance off-scene, then into phone):
>I just wanted you to know I'll be delayed a little longer, that's all.

277. CLOSE ON IDA (AT THE PHONE)

IDA:
>Hey—what's going on, Mildred?

278. CLOSE ON MILDRED

IDA'S VOICE (over phone):
>Are you in trouble?

MILDRED (hesitant):
>I'll . . . I'll tell you later. Keep the party going. (She hangs up.)

279. CLOSE ON IDA

as she hangs up the phone, looking worried. The CAM-
ERA PULLS BACK to reveal party in background and Monte
in foreground, with Veda.

MONTE:
Was that Mildred? (Ida nods.) Where is she?

IDA:
At the office. Something's going on . . . and I don't
like it. I think Mildred is having business trouble.

MONTE (smiling):
That can happen in the best of families . . .

IDA (puzzled):
Don't look now but you've got canary feathers all
over you . . .

Monte grins at her.

VEDA (bored):
Business . . . making money . . . that's all
Mother thinks about. Let's finish this dance,
Monte.

She starts toward the other room.

MONTE (to Ida, very politely):
Beauty calls. Excuse me.

IDA:
A pleasure.

As Monte goes away, the CAMERA MOVES IN on Ida. She
looks at Monte, and then at the phone, puzzled and
worried.

DISSOLVE TO:

280. INT. MILDRED'S OFFICE   NIGHT
At the desk is Mr. Jones, the accountant we have seen
before. His books are spread out all around him, and
Mildred is watching over his shoulder. Sitting at one

side, smoking nervously, is Wally Fay. Also in the room, is Wally's lawyer, complete with briefcase and papers.

LAWYER:
. . . I see no particular reason for going over this again. The situation is very clear. My clients demand an accounting. You must satisfy your creditors or show cause why control of Mildred's, Inc., should not be taken away from you. If you resist, your creditors force you into bankruptcy. It's as simple as that.

Mildred looks at Mr. Jones.

MILDRED:
Can they do it?

JONES:
I'm sorry, Mrs. Beragon.

MILDRED (straightening up wearily):
So am I. (To Wally.) Well, I've gone over everything. I haven't got a cent of ready cash in any of the restaurants.

281.   CLOSE   ON WALLY
as he rises and snuffs out his cigarette. The lawyer prepares to leave, putting away papers, etc.

WALLY (sincerely disturbed):
I wish it was different. I've been hoping you could scrape up enough money to get out of this mess. (He shrugs.) Anyhow, you can still manage the business.

282.   CLOSE   ON MILDRED

MILDRED (bitterly):
Thanks . . . that's pretty nice of you. Stealing my business out from under me and then letting me run it for you.

283. TWO SHOT MILDRED AND WALLY

WALLY:

> I'm not getting a bang out of doing this to you. I've
> no choice. You've been bleeding the business dry so
> you could live the way you have since Veda came
> home. You said that yourself.

MILDRED:

> I know.

WALLY:

> Okay. So you let a few bills go by. Then a few more.
> Until you're in real trouble. Now the creditors want
> your hide . . . and I can't hold them off. What did
> you expect? I'll bet that birthday party for Veda is
> costing you close to five thousand—

MILDRED:

> Six.

WALLY:

> Another month like this, and we'd all be out in the
> cold. As it is—

MILDRED:

> Only *I* am. Isn't that it?

WALLY (picking up his hat):

> I'm sorry. But it looks that way.

He goes toward the door, the lawyer preceding him out.
Wally turns to look at Mildred.

WALLY (continuing):

> If Monte hadn't forced the situation, you'd be all
> right.

MILDRED (startled):

> Monte? What's he got to do with this?

WALLY:

> I thought you knew. This was his idea. He wants to

sell his share of the business and I have to string
along with him or I'm out too. Didn't you know?[83]

Dazed, Mildred shakes her head. Wally's eyebrows go
up, and again he goes to the door.

WALLY (at the door):
You married him. I didn't.

Wally goes out through the deserted restaurant.

284.   TWO SHOT   MILDRED AND JONES   (MILDRED IN
FOREGROUND)
She is stunned by this startling news. Mr. Jones looks
sympathetic, as he starts closing the books.

MR. JONES (as he prepares to leave):
I'm very sorry that this should happen . . . and if I
do say it as I shouldn't, I think Mr. Beragon has
acted badly . . . (he starts out and stops to look
back at Mildred) very badly indeed. (Shaking his
head, he exits.)

Mildred goes to the window, dazed by the news she has
just heard. Then she turns and looks at her surround-
ings. She starts for the door of the restaurant.

284A.   FULL SHOT   RESTAURANT   (LOW ANGLE)   (LOW-KEY
LIGHTING)
SHOOTING across the breadth of the restaurant at
Mildred in the door of her office. She looks small and
defenseless. She paces the restaurant, smoking furiously, then comes to a sudden decision and goes back to
her office.

284B.·   MED. CLOSE   ON MILDRED
as she finishes dialing a number on the phone.

MILDRED:
Ida . . . this is Mildred. I want to speak with

Monte, please . . . He left? (A pause.) How long
ago? I see. (She hangs up slowly.)

IDA'S VOICE (urgent and worried; over phone):
Mildred—Mildred! (Her voice is cut off.)

Mildred opens the drawers of her desk rapidly until she
finds what she has been searching for—a gun. Without
looking at it, she puts it into her purse and then picks up
her hat and coat from a nearby chair.

DISSOLVE TO:

285.   INT. AUTOMOBILE (PROCESS)   RAINY NIGHT
as Mildred drives furiously. The windshield wipers
slap-slap rhythmically.

DISSOLVE TO:

286.   FULL SHOT EXT. BEACH HOUSE   NIGHT
which is lit up by the headlights of Mildred's car as it
comes in to a stop. Mildred gets out and goes to the door
of the house.

287.   MED. CLOSE (SHOOTING THROUGH OPEN
DOOR) MILDRED
as she pauses in the doorway, takes the gun from her
purse, and removes the safety. We hear the SOUND of
phonograph music, which is cut off—as is our sight of
Mildred—by the closing of the door.

DISSOLVE TO:

288.   INT. INSPECTOR'S OFFICE CLOSE SHOT MILDRED NIGHT
She speaks precisely and with no sign of emotion.

MILDRED:
I went in the house, and Monte was there alone
. . . I killed him.

The CAMERA PULLS BACK revealing the inspector's office.
The inspector at his desk is silent for an instant, watching Mildred. Then he speaks flatly.

PETERSON:

> You're a liar, Mrs. Beragon. (Rings a buzzer on his desk, then gets up.) We know you weren't alone in the house with Beragon . . . (Flips chemist's report.)[84] We have proof of that—and various other things. For instance— (SOUND of door opening off-scene.) We know who was there with you . . . (Nods toward the door, off.)

Mildred slowly turns her head in that direction. The CAMERA PANS to the door.

Veda is standing there with a detective and a heavyset police matron.

DETECTIVE:

> We picked her up at the airport . . . hadda drag her off a plane headed for Arizona. (Ruefully exhibiting some scratches.) She didn't like it much.

He goes out.

289. GROUP SHOT

The inspector looks at Veda levelly.

VEDA (elaborately casual):

> I don't understand . . .

PETERSON:

> You will. You see, we know all about it. Your mother told us . . . Why don't you tell us the rest? (Then viciously.) Why did you kill him?!

VEDA (shocked; to Mildred):

> You told?

MILDRED:

> Veda— I . . .

The inspector restrains her.

VEDA (in fury and fear):

> You promised not to tell! You promised! You said you'd help me get away!

MILDRED (heartsick):
Veda—don't say any more!

PETERSON (a grim smile):
Too late, Mrs. Beragon. Now we know the truth.
(To Veda.) It was *you*. (Consults the report.) You
left the party in Pasadena at approximately eleven-
thirty[85] . . . with Beragon. (A pause.) You were at
the beach house when your mother got there.

DISSOLVE TO:

290.   BERAGON'S BEACH HOUSE   CLOSE MILDRED'S FEET   NIGHT
as she walks across the living room floor to the stairs.

PETERSON'S VOICE (OVER SCENE):
I don't think you heard her come in. If you had,
maybe things would have been different . . .

The CAMERA PANS with her feet and then HOLDS at the
floor level, revealing Mildred as she goes down the
stairwell.

291.   INT. DEN   FULL SHOT   MONTE AND VEDA
with Veda FACING CAMERA. Monte's back is to us, but
his face is visible in the mirror behind the couple. They
kiss, then break apart, still embracing. Mildred appears
in the mirror. Monte notices the sudden frozen rigidity
of Veda, who is staring over his shoulder at Mildred. He
looks up, sees Mildred in the mirror, and then turns
slowly.

292.   GROUP SHOT
Mildred is staring at them. She is pointing the gun at
Monte.

293.   MONTE AND VEDA   SHOOTING PAST MILDRED
as Monte walks in on Mildred.

MONTE (easily):
We didn't expect you, Mildred—obviously. (Look-

ing at gun.) Uh—that's rather dangerous, isn't it? I
mean—it might go off.[86]

With a sudden quick movement he seizes her wrist with
his left hand and slaps the gun away with his right.
Then he releases her wrist.

MONTE (continuing; pleasantly):
    I don't like having guns pointed at me. I'm sorry if I
    hurt you.

MILDRED (her voice is dead):
    How long— (She swallows.) How long has this
    been going on?

VEDA:
    Since I came home. And even before. Monte and I
    have always understood each other—haven't we,
    Monte? Tell her.

MONTE:
    I guess we have, Veda.

VEDA (to her mother; brazenly):
    Monte and I are very much alike, you see.[87]

MILDRED:
    Yes. Yes, I see.

VEDA:
    I've got what I always wanted. Monte is going to
    divorce you and marry me. (Monte frowns sud-
    denly.) And there's nothing you can do about it.

MILDRED (quietly, as she goes to door):
    I guess not.[88]

She goes out. Monte turns to Veda.

MONTE:
    Where did you get the idea that I'm going to marry
    you?

VEDA:

Monte—don't joke like that.

MONTE:

I'm not joking. If you have any idea that I'm in love
with you, forget about it. (He shrugs.) You're nice,
Veda. Very pretty. But actually you're not my type.
(He turns away.)

VEDA (turns him back savagely):

Don't joke, Monte! You're going to marry me!

MONTE:

No, I'm not. (Scornfully.) How could you seriously
think that I'd marry a vicious brat like you?[89]

He shakes his head and goes toward the stairway. Veda
stares after him and then goes to where the gun is lying
on the floor, CAMERA WITH her.

DISSOLVE TO:

294.   INT. MILDRED'S CAR

Mildred is trying to start the car. We hear the SOUND of
shots, as in the opening. Mildred starts to get out of the
car.[90]

295.   FULL SHOT   AT DOORWAY

as the door opens and Veda runs out. Mildred stops her.

MILDRED:

What's the matter?

Holding onto Veda's wrist, Mildred pushes the girl
aside so that we can see into the room. Monte's body is
on the floor. Mildred goes in, preceding Veda, and
stands by the body. Veda closes the door, cutting off the
scene.

295A.   CLOSE   ON MILDRED   (BY BODY)   VEDA IN BACKGROUND

her back to the door.

VEDA:

> He said horrible things to me—didn't want me around anymore— He told me to get out. Then he laughed at me— He wouldn't stop laughing. I told him I'd kill him— He said I didn't have guts enough. (Wildly.) I didn't mean to do it! I didn't mean it, I tell you. But the gun kept going off—over and over again. And then he was lying there—looking at me— (she whispers) just looking at me.

296.   INT. BEACH HOUSE LIVING ROOM

Mildred is dazed by what her daughter has done.

MILDRED:

> He's dead. Monte's dead. I can't get you out of this, Veda.

Mildred starts for the phone. Suddenly Veda realizes her situation. She clutches at her mother.

VEDA:

> You've got to help me. Give me money to get away—and time— I've got to get away before they find him. Please . . .

Avoiding her daughter's touch, Mildred picks up the phone and dials.

VEDA (frightened):

> What are you going to do?

MILDRED (into phone):

> Give me the police department . . .

VEDA:

> No! No, Mother! Think what will happen to me if they find me. Think what will happen . . .

MILDRED:

> I don't care anymore, Veda . . .

VEDA (beginning to cry with terror):

> Yes, you do—yes, you do. You can't let me down

now— It's as much your fault as mine— Give me a chance.

PHONE VOICE (on filter; coming OVER):
Santa Monica Police Department. O'Grady speaking.

VEDA:
You've got to help me. Help me, Mother! Just this once— I'll change— I promise I will. I'll be different— I'll be good. Just give me another chance! It's your fault I'm the way I am— Help me!

PHONE VOICE (with irritation):
Hello? Hello? Hello!

Slowly, Mildred hangs up the phone.

DISSOLVE TO:

297.   CLOSE   ON MILDRED
with the CAMERA PULLING BACK to reveal her in the inspector's office.

MILDRED:
I thought maybe . . . in a way . . . it was *my* fault. So I tried to help her. I wanted to take the blame for it.

PETERSON (shaking his head):
Not this time, Mrs. Beragon. This time your daughter pays for her own mistake . . .[91]

He motions to the matron, who helps Veda up from the chair. Veda looks at her mother, turns away, and goes out with the matron.

PETERSON:
You can go now. We'll call you when we want you (To Ed.) Let those others go too.

MILDRED (to Bert):
Take me home, Bert.

They go out together.

235

298. FULL SHOT   SIDE CORRIDOR
as Mildred and Bert walk toward the main corridor,
looking only at each other. The CAMERA PANS them past
Wally and Ida just coming out of the other room and
then HOLDS on Wally and Ida.
   Wally starts to call after Mildred, but sees that she
doesn't notice him.

WALLY (to Ida):
   You know something . . . I'm getting a little dis-
   couraged about her. (Indicating Mildred.) I'm beginning to think I haven't got a chance.

IDA (dryly):
   You're just a pessimist.

WALLY (looking Ida over carefully):
   Say, how about you cooking some breakfast for me?

IDA (as they start away):
   Okay. I'll give you some scrambled eggs . . . but
   that's all. I hate to wrestle in the morning.

299. TRUCKING SHOT   MILDRED AND BERT
as they come into the main corridor. Sunlight is streaming through the windows. Mildred stops.

MILDRED:
   What will happen to her?

BERT (shrugs):
   She's very young. There was no premeditation.
   Juries think of these things. (He shrugs again.)
   Maybe a few years. Why?

MILDRED:
   I'm still her mother.

Mildred looks up at him and smiles a little. They go on
out of scene past the CAMERA which HOLDS on the
scrubwoman we saw earlier, who has just finished with

her work for the night. She puts the brushes and rags into the pail, gets to her feet, and then walks away down the corridor.

FADE OUT

THE END

Notes to the Screenplay

1 The titles in the film appear as described in MacDougall's first draft: "FADE IN UNDER TITLES THE SURF (BY MOONLIGHT) at Malibu. Waves come ashore heavily, as they do at night, and wash away TITLES as they appear."

The opening shots of the script are replaced by the following in film: (1) a long shot of the beach house with ocean and pier in background and a car with lights on parked beside the house; dissolve to (2) a closer shot of the same; (3) Monte before a mirror, facing camera. He is startled; shots ring out and hit him; camera pans with him as he falls. He says, "Mildred." He is dead. A gun is tossed beside him. The camera pans to the mirrored wall, now showing bullet holes, and toward a door, which shuts. We do not see who exits. In a long shot the car leaves, the driver unrecognizable. Dissolve to overhead shot of the Santa Monica Pier. Camera dollies in on Mildred in a fur coat, her back to us, as she walks down the foggy pier.

2 Mildred's tears are minimal in the film. Crawford plays the role less weepily.

3 This script marks the first appearance of Wally as Wally Fay. In earlier versions and in the book, he is Wally Burgan. The name was presumably changed to avoid confusion with Monte's surname, Beragon.

4 As Wally accompanies her inside, he says, "You know, buying this joint was the smartest move I ever made." When they seat themselves, he asks a waiter, "Give us a couple of drinks, will you, Tony?" The camera pans to reveal Miriam (scene 259) singing on the stage in the background.

5 The action and dialogue of the rest of scene 25 are different in the film. Mildred and Wally descend the spiral staircase to the den; the camera pans to the body of Monte on the living room floor. We hear their voices off screen:

MILDRED: Nervous, Wally?

WALLY: Cold— (he pauses) temporarily!

There is a dissolve from the body to drinks being mixed.

MILDRED: Isn't this more comfortable?

238

WALLY: Yeah, I guess so.

MILDRED: What's the matter?

6 In the film Mildred resists the kiss and knocks her own drink on the floor. Then coldly she says, "I'm sorry."

7 Mildred huddles against the mirror in her room. As Wally talks, the camera cuts between her and him in the bar. She is clearly frightened. The emphasis, particularly with the *noir* lighting, is on her; Wally's information, though vital, is somewhat reduced to background. Mildred is planning her move. In the film, the following action and dialogue replace the rest of scene 26, scene 27, and Wally's first speech in scene 28:

WALLY: But I'm glad you didn't get sore at me the way I took you over the hurdles, Mildred. I didn't mean to cut up your business the way I did. I just got started and couldn't stop. I can't help myself. I see an angle, right away I start cutting myself a piece of throat. It's an instinct. (Shot of door closing.) With me being smart's a disease. Know what I mean? (The door shuts.) Hey, Mildred. Hurry up. You know I don't like to drink alone. Hey! Say something. This one-sided conversation is beginning to bore me.

Exterior shot of beach with house in background. Mildred is running along the beach.

8 Wally adds, "But don't get me sore." This is a typical on-the-set change. Hereafter, only the most significant changes will be noted.

9 Scenes 29–31 are visually much more dramatic in the film. Wally tries Mildred's door. It is locked. He looks up the striking spiral staircase; from the top of it we see him ascend it. In a long shot we see him illuminated by a passing car's lights, and then we see his shadow in gigantic relief as he pounds on the locked front door to get out of the house.

10 A taxi, not a bus, lets Mildred off at the Pasadena house. The tone of the movie is much more elegant than that of MacDougall's script. The interior shot of the mansion's foyer emphasizes its vastness.

11 After Veda's exit, Mildred says to the two detectives, "Can't you tell me what's happened?" One of them says, "We'd better go." At the door Mildred again asks, "What's wrong? What's the matter?" The detective says, "I didn't want to say anything in front of your daughter. It's your husband. He's been murdered." She receives the information with a startled look and says, "Murdered?"

12 In scenes 57–59 in the film, we see the floor pattern with the emblem of the Hall of Justice. Max Steiner's swelling music sets the scene.

The camera pans to show the detectives entering with Mildred. They go to a door marked Criminal Division, Room 220.

13 Scene 61 is handled more fluidly in the film. Ida is already seated in the office. The camera pans to reveal her to Mildred's gaze. She leans forward to greet Mildred, but is restrained by a policeman. She toughly replies, "Look, I bruise easy." The intercom buzzes and the man, Ed, says, "Ida Corwin." He motions her into the interior office. She rises to go and Mildred gazes after her. The camera pans to show her meeting Wally, who is now entering. Their paths cross. Ida: "What is this, the class reunion?" Wally (muttering): "Looks like it. (He stops to speak to Mildred.) I'll have a tough time talking my way out of this."

14 The end of scene 62 and scene 63 are different, again more fluid. The camera pans with the reporter to the water cooler, and Bert is seen entering. Bert: "Sorry, Mildred." Ed: "No talking." Mildred is silent. She doesn't say his name as in the script, but she is shocked. There is a reaction shot of Bert, lit in *noir* style. He looks guilty.

15 The scene is somewhat different in the film. The clock shows the time as 2:45. Ed says, "Paper, lady?" and Mildred replies, "No, thank you." An echo accentuates voices and normal sounds. Mildred keeps glancing around nervously. There are disturbing noises: a pencil sharpener, whistling, the sharp opening of a newspaper. Finally a buzzer sounds. Ed and Mildred enter the office where she is introduced to Inspector Peterson.

16 Mildred's voice-over speech was rewritten for the film: "Bert was out. They weren't partners anymore. That day when Bert came home he was out of a job." It made no sense, in scene 90, for Mildred to nag Bert to get a job, unless her statement that he didn't tell about losing his job was stricken from the screenplay.

17 In the film Mildred adds, "I married Bert when I was seventeen. I never knew any other kind of life. Just cooking and washing and having children. (The camera pans to the picture on the piano.) Two girls. Veda and Kay."

18 This speech is not in the film. With this script Kay gets a new name. In the book and elsewhere she is Ray.

19 Mildred's reply in the film softens her nagging: "I know you will, Bert. I was just trying to help."

20 In the film the exchange is expanded: "Baking cakes and making pies for the neighbors. That's where I got it. I earned it." "That's right. Throw it up at me that I can't support my own family."

21 "Clip her one" becomes "slap her right in the face." Despite

Mildred's reply, she later does just that, and still later Veda does the same to Mildred.

22 Bert says "isn't right to" instead of "isn't natural." The film plays down any hint of unnaturalness in Mildred's love for Veda, but it still condemns to some extent her displacing Bert in her affection for Veda.

23 In the film Mildred adds "before either one of us. Maybe that's right and maybe it's wrong, but that's the way it is." The question of rightness echoes Bert's remarks and underlines Mildred's own involvement in her fate. The pause on the line suggests that it is central to understanding the film. Bert may be at fault too, but it is principally Mildred who upsets the harmony of the family by her excessive love for Veda and her placing of her children over Bert.

24 Scenes 98A–101 are not in the film. In an earlier draft Monte actually gives Veda a ride home and tells her to come around again when she is older. Both the children see their father leave between scenes 103 and 104.

25 In the film the game is football, not softball. Kay is playing center and directing a play. All the others are boys. "Pass it," she calls out. Veda looks on, upset. She grabs Kay and leads her off saying, "For goodness sake." Kay responds, "Aw, I ain't done nothing. You never let anybody have fun."

26 She adds, "We'll have to get along by ourselves now." Veda asks, "What did you and father quarrel about?" In the preceding speech Kay instead says, "You mean Dad's not coming home anymore? Doesn't he like us?" In scenes 102, 104, and 105 the film gives Kay more to do, making her rather lovable and in sharp contrast to Veda.

27 The dialogue in the film begins:
KAY: You ought to do something about your sit-down.
VEDA: What's wrong with it?
KAY: It sticks out.
VEDA: It's the dress. It's awful cheap material.

28 Veda adds, "It's horrible. How could she have bought me such a thing?" Mildred overhears outside, is hurt, and goes back downstairs.

29 Wally's and Mildred's lines in the film are: "Bert must be crazy! (He exclaims this to himself and laughs at his good fortune.) I never did mind being around you, Mildred." "You don't by any chance hear opportunity knocking, do you?"

30 Wally says, "I like Scotch." Mildred replies knowingly, "I know what you like."
31 Wally adds, "You know I wouldn't drop dead at the idea of marrying you." Mildred's reply is simply, "Quit kidding, will you?" It is easy to imagine Crawford's objecting to the line in the screenplay.
32 In the film the next exchange becomes:

WALLY: Yeah, easy on the ice . . . No soda?
MILDRED: Sorry, Bert never had it around.
WALLY: We'll take care of that . . . Say when. (As though he were making the drink for her.)
MILDRED: None for me. I'm not used to it.
WALLY: Take care of that too.
MILDRED: You're pretty sure of yourself, aren't you?
WALLY: You've got to get educated, Mildred . . .

The rest of Wally's speech contains key lines from the book, delivered to Mildred by Lucy Gessler, her neighbor and confidante, as encouragement to try to hook Wally. After passing through the mouths of a number of characters in the various scripts, by the final screenplay they come from Wally's.

Much is made in the film of Mildred's movement from nondrinker to drinker. In present time she is taking her liquor straight, and the problem is linked to her disillusionment with men. It is also an index of her growing toughness, her movement away from home and into the business world with its tensions. It is finally linked to her unhappiness about Veda.

33 The following exchange ends the scene:

MILDRED: Then quit howling! I know you romantic guys. One crack about the beautiful moon and you're off to the races.
WALLY: Especially when it looks like a sure thing. (He starts to kiss her shoulder.)
MILDRED (evades him and gets up): Here we go again.
WALLY: Did I do something wrong?
MILDRED: You'd better go, Wally.
WALLY: No dice, huh?
MILDRED: Good night.
WALLY: Well, no dice, no dice. (He finishes his drink and she hands him his straw hat.) You can't shoot a guy for trying. I just thought maybe if . . . Ah, Mildred, I was only kidding. I wouldn't pull any cheap trick like that on you. You know that.
MILDRED: Yes, I know. (Knowingly and skeptically.)
WALLY: Why, I . . .

MILDRED (opens the door to show him out): I said good night, Wally.

WALLY: Okay, okay. Round one goes to Mildred Pierce.

MILDRED: There won't be any round two.

WALLY (as he leaves, his head in the door): We live in hope. I'll keep on trying.

MILDRED: I know, once a week. (Resignedly but with some humor.)

WALLY (he holds up two fingers and makes the correction she made in scene 9): Twice a week.

Mildred shakes her head, knowing it's impossible to stop him, and closes the door.

Mildred is both strong and good humored in this scene. It's one of her most likable moments in the film.

34 Mildred is in bed, looking at ads for jobs in the paper, and instead says, "I had to get a job, any kind. I had no experience in the business world but I had to get a job."

35 The montage sequence is much shorter in the film, opening with Mildred's moving legs and a few despairing remarks and including only the man behind the wicket. Extremely economical, it condenses the screenplay version as well as several elaborate ones in previous scripts and the book, but diminishes the image of immense difficulty. Mildred's glamourous appearance in a stylish hat also detracts from her suffering.

36 Scenes 132–36 are changed and cut considerably. Mr. Chris is not in the film, and scenes showing Mildred learning the business and getting the pie concession are truncated. The film version follows: The waitresses stop bickering. Mildred reacts, contemplates, and makes her decision.

CUSTOMER (to Ida): How about some service?

IDA: Oh, I'm sorry. I'll have someone take care of you right away.

There is still more quarreling among the waitresses.

IDA (to the waitresses, strongly): You mind your own business. (She goes back to Mildred.) Sorry to leave you like that but we're so shorthanded. And now this. Let's see, you wanted tea?

MILDRED (decisively): No, I want a job.

IDA: What?

MILDRED: Well, you seem to need help. And I want a job.

IDA (hand on hip): Did you ever work in a restaurant before?

MILDRED (shakes her head; diffidently): No.

IDA (decisively): Follow me. (Then to Mildred, who follows hurriedly and nearly bumps a waitress.) Kind of a nervous gal, aren't you?

MILDRED: I'm just a little overanxious, I guess.

IDA: You wanta watch that. It's tough on dishes.

Dissolve to Ida taking down uniform.

IDA: Personally, I don't think you're the type for the work. But against my better judgment I'll give you a trial. Now you need white shoes. Ask for nurses' regulation. Any of the stores. Two ninety-five. (She sits down on the bench outside the locker and lights a cigarette.) We furnish your uniform but it comes off your first check. Three ninety-five. You get it at cost and keep it laundered. If you don't suit us, we charge you twenty-five cents on the uniform—that comes off your check too. Keep your own tips. Here, have your tea. (Warmly.)

MILDRED (now in uniform; she takes the tea): Thank you. (With warmth and gratitude.) What's your name?

IDA: Ida. What's yours?

MILDRED: Mildred Pierce. (She smiles and drinks her tea.)

Dissolve to a busy kitchen with the cook ladling out food to hurrying waitresses. There is a babel of orders. Mildred is third in line placing orders.

MILDRED (reaching the cook): Two chicken dinners, one without gravy.

IDA (intruding): Two chickens, hold one gravy. (To Mildred.) You can't say "without." You got to say "hold."

Dissolve to plates being cleaned off table with uneaten pies.

MILDRED (VOICE-OVER): I learned the restaurant business. I learned it the hard way. In three weeks I was a good waitress.

Shot of Mildred rushing to kitchen to order.

MILDRED (shouting): One chicken. Hold veg. Club sandwich. Roast beef. Hold one. Club and salad.

MILDRED (VOICE-OVER): In six weeks I felt as though I'd worked in a restaurant all my life. (Shot of Mildred with customers getting up from table.) And in three months I was one of the best waitresses in the place. I took tips and was glad to get them. (Mildred is now clearing the table and picking up the tips. Dissolve to Mildred putting a pie in the oven at home.) And at home I baked pies for the restaurant.

MILDRED (talking to black maid Lottie in the kitchen): Those'll be done in another couple minutes. (She consults her order sheet.) Let's see now. We have a dozen peach, a dozen berry, a dozen pumpkin, and a dozen cherry. Now when we finish the apple, we can quit for the night.

LOTTIE: I don't know how you keep it up, Mrs. Pierce. Honest I don't. Now I sleep all morning but you go down to that restaurant and work and work, just like you been sleeping all night—only you ain't.

MILDRED: It keeps me thin.

LOTTIE: Beg pardon!

MILDRED: Um! (Assenting.)

LOTTIE: Don't do nothing for me! (She checks her arms and body for fat.)

Dissolve to the bankbook.

37 The rest of scene 139 is not in the film.

38 Here he eyes her legs and says, "I haven't seen enough of you lately." She pulls down her skirt. The line about the gams comes later.

39 Fifteen hundred cars becomes five hundred, and the next two speeches are omitted.

40 This script has no previous reference to a picture. The statement is a carry-over from MacDougall's first draft, which calls for a number of pictures early in the film and revisits them in the manner of *Citizen Kane*. Another such carry-over is found in scene 219.

41 Wally adds, "And remember, let me do the talking." The line explains his taking some of her lines in the next scene. As they leave, the two are silhouetted against the wall. Mildred is exuberant and cries out, "Wally, you're wonderful!" Wally holds his hand up to her mouth and says, "Uh-uh. This is all business, remember."

42 Mildred prepares to answer his question: "Yes, I have it all," but Wally, according to his earlier remark, speaks the next lines that are assigned to her in the script.

43 They have a drink together, and Wally already clearly recognizes that a relationship is unlikely. As they drink to their deal he says with a chuckle, "Hey, how about Uncle Wally, here?"

44 The talk about Mrs. Biederhof is omitted.

45 Instead of the preceding three lines, the following takes place:

BERT (angrily): I want to know more about this deal with Wally Fay, a whole lot more.

MILDRED: Well, what have you got to do with that?

BERT: You're my wife, aren't you?

MILDRED: Yes, but you certainly seem to forget about it. Especially when it comes to Maggie Biederhof.

BERT: Well, what about you and Wally Fay?

MILDRED (shocked and hurt): You should know better than that.

46 Mildred adds, "And there's very little you can do about it. I don't need your permission."

47 The camera pans to the record player and we see Monte and Mildred kissing in the wall mirror—the same one in which we witnessed Monte's slaying at the opening.

48 The character Pancho is omitted. The scene opens with Mildred's putting an apron on Wally.

WALLY (startled): What is this? I'm an executive.

MILDRED: You're now vice-president in charge of the potatoes. Will you pick them up and put them in the fat for me?

LOTTIE (observing Wally): You look very pretty, Mr. Fay.

WALLY: Thank you.

LOTTIE: Not at all.

Wally does a double take.

49 Through a window Wally sees Monte arrive carrying a box of orchids. Mildred is still giving Wally instructions.

MILDRED: Don't let the potatoes burn.

WALLY: I was just asking a question. (He mutters.)

MILDRED (to a waitress): Dorothy, don't ever go in like that. Put some more potatoes on. (She puts more potatoes on her plate.)

DOROTHY: You'll never make any money that way.

MILDRED: It's all right, as long as the customers are satisfied.

LOTTIE (with excitement): This is just like my wedding night. So exciting!

Out in front, this exchange follows (scene 203 is omitted):

MONTE: Will you please see that Mrs. Pierce gets these flowers?

IDA: Can I tell her your name or is it a secret?

MONTE: Tell her they came from an old gypsy fortune teller.

IDA: Well, sit down and read a teacup. I'll see if she's busy. (She exits and appears at the kitchen door to deliver flowers.) Hey, Mildred, real live orchids.

MILDRED: For me?

IDA: Uh-huh.

WALLY: Orchids? Say, what is this? Who're they from? (He is working in his apron.)

IDA: From an old gypsy fortune teller with beautiful brown eyes.

LOTTIE (does a double take on the words "brown eyes"): Beg pardon!

MILDRED: Put them in the icebox for me, will you, Wally?

Wally takes the flowers, prepares to put them in the icebox, but hesitates before a can marked Refuse and very deliberately drops them in.

In all the Monte-Mildred-Wally scenes, Wally's jealousy is more underscored in the film, as is Mildred's unromantic treatment of him.

50 Wally adds, "A third of this joint belongs to me." Perhaps this line was inserted to make credible Wally's manipulations (with Monte) of Mildred at the end. Some hinting of it seems to go on when Bert discusses the divorce in scene 164. But this is the first we hear of his actually owning a share of the business; how—or why—he got it we do not know. In the book Wally takes over as manager for Mildred's creditors; he does not own her business.

This scene also continues somewhat differently. Monte congratulates Wally about owning a share of the successful business and Wally proposes a deal to Monte. "Tell you another little business proposition that might interest you. You know that orange grove you got?" Monte interrupts; Wally is probably too crude for him. "Save it till later. Well, here's to success."

51 After scene 205 there is a shot of the busy restaurant, a dolly into the cook's revolving order wheel with the wheel full, and a quick time lapse with a dolly back and the lights going off. The same wheel is now still and empty.

Monte and Veda are at the jukebox. Monte selects a record and they dance. Wally is excluded and stands on the sidelines with a drink. He appears a bit drunk and later hums the tune they dance to.

VEDA: That's a wonderful piece!

WALLY: You know, Beragon, all you need now is a pair of bobby-socks.

MONTE (while dancing with Veda): Maybe Veda will lend me a pair.

There is general laughter. Mildred enters, exhausted. Ida is at the cash register.

IDA: Well, the last customer just folded his tent.

MILDRED: That's good. We've only got one chicken left.

IDA: Put my initials on that.

MILDRED (sitting down and rubbing her feet): Oh, I'm so tired I don't know whether I'm walking on my feet or my ankles. You must be dead.

IDA: If I am, just bury me with this. (She tosses some money around.)

MILDRED (looks over at Veda and Monte dancing): I wish I felt the way they do.

Wally sips his drink and sings "No Other One" with the jukebox.

52 Wally adds, "Besides, I want to take *you* home." Mildred pleads, "Wally, look, I've got to close up. I'll go home with Ida. Please, c'mon." Wally is more persistent in the film and more constantly rebuffed. His fears are realized, since Mildred is soon romantic with Monte.

53 Here Wally leaves with Veda and hesitates as he looks at Ida, who is standing on a chair after having fixed something on the wall. She is now adjusting her skirt. Ida: "Leave something on me. I might catch cold." Wally: "I'm just thinking . . . (Mumbling.) Not about you."

Wally's bitterness toward Mildred keeps coming out at Ida in the film. Instead of moving toward an Ida-Wally relationship as the script does, the film increases their antagonism.

54 The flash of headlights and scene 208 are not in the film. Bert arrives later.

55 Instead of broken glass on the floor, Curtiz offers a semi-tableau, a punctuation shot, of Mildred and Monte on either side of Bert, looking aghast at his violence. This nicely dovetails into the theme of the first flashback: Bert as murderer.

56 What this information is remains a bit puzzling. Apparently it is Ida's information that Mildred, Monte, and Veda were all at the beach house. In earlier drafts the information seemed to be fingerprints of Veda, which, though we were not told here, led the detectives to stopping her at the airport. Here they simply seem to act upon her having been at the scene of the crime, although that would give them little reason to suspect that she is the murderer. When Louise Pierson was writing her script, she wrote to Wald and Curtiz saying that she did not know what the new information was and suspected it might be traces of Veda's hair.

57 From here on this scene varies considerably. Wally is much more hurt and angry at being rebuffed.

MILDRED: No?

WALLY: No. Look, I made this business for you with my own hands. I chiseled Monte out of the deed and I got the banks to give you credit. And believe me, that wasn't easy. I've conned everybody until I'm blue in the face and for what? So you can have a lap dog named Beragon?

MILDRED: Take it easy, Wally.

WALLY: When you walked out on Bert, it was okay with me. I was glad to see you get some sense in your head. And now you're falling for a guy that's a worse foul ball than Bert ever thought of being.

MILDRED: That's none of your business.

WALLY: I say it is. I'm not the type that likes to be left out in the cold. The only reason I helped you was so that I could be around when you changed your mind about me. Maybe I was wrong.

MILDRED: Maybe you were.

WALLY: You're making a mistake, Mildred. This Beragon is no good. He'll bleed you dry.

MILDRED (suddenly stopping and shifting the tone): Suppose I'm in love with him.

These additions adumbrate two major themes: that Wally was never acting just for business but with the hopes that he could win Mildred, and that the business is built on shaky legal foundations. When Wally finds out that there is no possibility of romance, his anger easily becomes revenge upon Mildred. Unlike the Mildred of the book, the film's Mildred has not achieved the business on her own, even though she may think she has.

58 Wally bitterly says to Ida, "I hate all women." She rather mockingly replies, "My, my," and he retorts even more strongly, "Thank goodness you're not one." Again Wally takes out his bitterness toward Mildred on Ida.

59 Mildred then tells Ida what happened. "I just told him I was in love with Monte Beragon." "Are you?" Ida asks. Then Mildred thoughtfully says, "I thought I was once . . . but not now."

These lines seem to be meant honestly. Perhaps they are here to prepare for Mildred's dismissal of Monte in the next scene. The proximity of the two dismissals, however, makes Mildred look more opportunistic than she probably is. Her statement to Wally about loving Monte now looks like a lie—here softened by this remark about her unsureness. But the suspicion that she has engineered a ploy to get rid of Wally and gain more control lingers. That is not the case, but such are the problems of condensation.

60 Instead of this line, Mildred quickly changes the subject. "Did you bring the Laguna Beach and Las Villas statements with you?" Ida rises and complies, "They're over here."

61 The exchange between Ida and Monte at the beginning of scene 230 comes here in the film. It sets up Monte's dismissal in the next scene, but Mildred's statement to Ida that she doesn't love Monte has hardly been that strong. And if it had been, it would make her a

liar to Wally when she told him she loved Monte. Again, these seem problems in condensing a complicated plot.

62 "Ted Forrester" is changed to "Monte" (and at the end of the scene she does not refer to a date with Ted). This lays the groundwork for their later romance. The sophisticated cigarette case makes a significant gift from Monte to Veda as she enters his more glamourous, adult, and elegant world.

63 The film's Veda is too sophisticated for horn honking.

64 Monte does not accuse Mildred of jealousy.

65 Mildred adds, "I blame it all on you," and Monte's next speech begins with "I don't think you know Veda very well."

66 The film omits some lines in the preceding exchange and becomes:

    MONTE: Yes, I take money from you, Mildred. But not enough to make me like kitchens or cooks. They smell of grease.

    MILDRED: I don't notice you shrinking away from a fifty-dollar bill because it happens to smell of grease.

    MONTE: Take it easy, Mildred.

67 There are no tears in Mildred's eyes as she watches Monte leave. Scenes 231 and 232 are omitted. Instead, the dissolve takes place on Mildred's face framed in the colonial-style windows.

68 Scene 233 opens with Wally at the bar opening a champagne bottle. A woman customer at a nearby table looks on. "I'd like some of that," she says. "You've got to work for it, kid," he replies. As he leaves he says to her, "Keep your motor running," and the camera pans with him as he goes over to Veda and Ted at their table. Ted and Veda's dialogue in scene 234 is omitted.

69 Curtiz holds the camera for a long while on Veda and Wally exchanging knowing glances. That they are going to exploit the innocent Ted is underlined. The next two scenes, 240–241, are omitted.

70 At this point Wally says, "My client feels—and I am in complete accord with her—that she has been irrep—" He stumbles on the word. Williams helps him: "Irreparably?" Wally replies, "*Unduly* damaged," and picks up the screenplay dialogue at "there's one little formality."

71 Wally replies indignantly but with a shade of mockery and triumph, "That's no way to talk about a baby."

72 Instead, Wally says, "I guess that's about all. You can make out the check to Mrs. For— to Miss Veda Pierce."

73 This line about money is placed after Veda's next diatribe to Mildred.

74 Mildred's line in the film is less stinging: "It's just a little habit I

picked up from men." Ida replies simply, "That's the way it is, Mildred. I never yet met a man . . ." The omission of Ida's significant lines about men's envy of women seriously robs the film of an important social theme. Mildred also appears more bitter from failed romance than angry at men. The focus is shifted away from the problem of sexual equality.

75 In the film, this dialogue follows Ida's answering the telephone (Bert's voice is heard as if over the phone):

IDA (to Mildred): It's Bert. He's been calling every day on the hour for a month.

MILDRED (taking the phone): Hello, Bert. How are you?

BERT: Fine. How are you?

MILDRED: I'm fine. Yes, I just got back this morning.

BERT: How about dinner tomorrow night?

MILDRED: Tomorrow night? (She hesitates.) Well, of course, I want to have dinner with you. But what about Mrs. Biederhof? Maybe she wouldn't like . . .

BERT: She's married.

MILDRED (incredulously): She is?

BERT: Yeah, a couple of weeks ago.

MILDRED: Okay. You pick me up at the house at seven thirty.

BERT: Swell.

MILDRED: Good-bye. (She hangs up. To Ida.) Imagine that. Somebody married Mrs. Biederhof.

IDA: Well, that's a novelty. Remind me to bake a cake. How's Bert?

Bert is not only rehabilitated with a job; he is free to come back to Mildred. Does Mrs. Biederhof's marriage signify that he never had an affair with her? Or that it was lukewarm at most? We are led to believe whatever we like. Mildred's warm response also shows that her love for Bert is being rekindled, or perhaps that it was really always there.

At the end of scene 254 Ida lifts her glass and says, "To the men we have loved." They click glasses and she adds, "The stinkers."

76 In the film Mildred is less carping.

MILDRED: I never did like this place. Does Wally still own it?

BERT: Yeah. (To a waiter.) Two rum collins, please.

MILDRED: I still don't know why you insisted on coming here.

BERT: I thought it was a good idea at the time. Now I'm not so sure.

Veda then enters in costume and sings her song ("Billy McCoy was a musical boy . . .") and the sailors wolf-whistle at her. Miriam and Veda's dialogue in scene 259 is omitted.

77 Veda does not put her arms around Mildred. Instead, she is distant and cold. Mildred's speech that follows is instead, "If I could give you the kind of life Monte taught you, would you be willing to come home then?" Veda replies, "But you couldn't, could you, Mother?" This provides a closer link to Monte and what she actually does to secure Veda's love.

78 The film makes more of Mildred's increased drinking. As Monte begins to fix her a drink, she startles him by saying, "I prefer it straight."

79 Bert is seen in silhouette, seated in a chair and reading a newspaper. Then the paper is crumpled angrily and tossed aside. The paragraph that follows the wedding announcement is omitted, as is Mildred's voice-over.

80 Lottie has some confusion about answering and insists that Bert wait. Mildred's meeting Bert is also changed considerably.

LOTTIE: It's nice to see you again, Mr. Pierce.

BERT: It's nice to see you, Lottie.

LOTTIE: It's such a long, long time. Follow me. (Then she motions him back.) Oh, no, no. I'm supposed to announce everybody. You stay there. Pardon me. (She approaches a study where Mildred is at work behind a desk. Loudly.) Mr. Albert Pierce.

MILDRED (rising and passing Lottie): Not so loud.

LOTTIE: No?

MILDRED (warmly): Hello, Bert. Nice to see you.

BERT: Thanks, Mildred. I was just driving by and thought maybe I'd drop in and say hello. Hope you don't mind.

MILDRED: Oh, of course not. Come in and sit down. Would you like a drink?

BERT: No, thanks, my hours are too long. I can't do it these days. (He eyes the mansion.)

MILDRED: Let's sit over here.

BERT: My, this is quite a nifty place.

MILDRED: Yes, we just finished redecorating. You didn't come to the wedding.

81 Bert stands in the background and does not leave without saying good-bye. Veda says, "Mother, this is a beautiful place." Mildred goes over to Bert and thanks him: "Bert, I'm very grateful." While she is talking to Bert, the camera pans to catch Monte entering and spotting Veda. He says with joy, "I don't believe it. I simply don't believe it!"

82 The film offers more comic business with Lottie. Instead of

"definitely," she says, "Well, it's the newest we could get," and then exclaims to a butler, "Isn't this a beautiful night? I just love parties, don't you?" "I beg your pardon!" he haughtily corrects her. Lottie is flustered and utters, "Thank you kindly." Her confusion persists as she picks up the phone and seems to forget which end to speak through.

83 Apparently Monte has talked Wally into joining forces with him to gain cash. But why Monte would do this is not clear; Mr. Jones says it was very unexpected. If Monte had no serious interest in Veda, there seems no reason for him to do it. Is this one of Wally's schemes, akin to the deal he proposed on the opening night of the restaurant? The business matters in the film are quite confusing. Faulkner tried to solve them in his screenplay—also giving a three-way ownership—and had to devote most of the script to them. It is also unclear whether Wally acts out of spite or merely instinct, as he claimed in the beginning (note 7). Unlike the book, the focus is shifted away from Mildred's extravagance, foolishness, and debts for Veda's sake and onto the double-dealing of Wally and Monte.

84 The film does not mention a chemist's report and omits the rest of Peterson's speech. The chemist's report obviously suggests finger-prints as his confirmation that Veda committed the murder. The film offers a new proof, and it seems to confirm the theory that Peterson knew from the start that Mildred had not committed the murder. Several recent interpretations of the film rest on this bit of Peterson's new dialogue: "You see, Mrs. Beragon, we've had a slant on you from the beginning. You were the key. We had to put the pressure on you. Well, the key turned. The door opened and there was the murderer." Here the door opens and the two detectives bring in Veda.

85 In the film Peterson adds, "Your mother left her office at eleven forty-five. You were already at the beach house when she got there shortly after midnight. Isn't that right, Mrs. Beragon?" After great difficulty Mildred replies, "Yes. I didn't know Veda was there when I came in. I expected Monte to be alone." Dissolve to shot of Mildred descending the spiral staircase and standing at the bottom in shadows. She sees Monte kissing Veda in silhouette on the bar. They see her and emerge from the shadows.

86 The lines about the gun are omitted. Mildred has not drawn the gun at this point in the film.

87 Veda is particularly vicious here. "It's just as well you know. I'm

glad you know." The lines about their being alike are omitted and Veda adds, "He never loved you. It's always been me."

88 Mildred's weak "I guess not" is omitted. She says loudly, "Veda," then she deliberates and is about to withdraw the gun from her pocket when Monte approaches and says, "Mildred, use your head. This won't solve anything." Then he wrests the gun from her hand and it drops to the floor. Mildred turns and exits up the staircase.

89 "Vicious brat" becomes "rotten little tramp."

90 After this scene occurs the famous missing "reverse" angle shot (actually it initiates the reverse shot of Monte's being shot). This is the shot that was withheld at the opening. Veda is shown firing the gun at Monte. The shot we have seen before follows—Monte's being shot and falling, saying, "Mildred." Mildred enters the house and Veda says, "It's Monte."

91 The film substitutes the following for the remainder of the script:
PETERSON: Okay, book her.
Veda is led to the left. Mildred rises and they speak. Mildred embraces her but Veda, while not completely rejecting her, wants it to be brief and cool.
MILDRED: Veda, I'm sorry. I did the best I could.
VEDA: Don't worry about me, Mother. I'll get by.
They lead her off
PETERSON (to the detectives): See that those others are released. (He raises a blind. To Mildred.) We need some fresh air in here. Looks like a nice morning. (Sunlight pours into the room.) You can go now. We'll call you when we want you. You know, Mrs. Beragon, there are times when I regret being a police officer. (He helps her on with her fur coat.)
Mildred exits, then sees Bert at the end of the hallway. He is waiting for her. Together they walk out of the building into an arch through which the sunshine floods. There is upbeat music. At their right two scrubwomen work on the floor.
   None of the Wally-Ida dialogue is in the script. Their relationship has soured too much for it. Nor is there any discussion about the fate of Veda. The emphasis is on the restored relationship of Bert and Mildred. The mood is suddenly very positive.

Production Credits

Produced by	Jerry Wald
Directed by	Michael Curtiz
Screenplay by	Ranald MacDougall
Based on the novel by	James M. Cain
Music by	Max Steiner
Director of Photography	Ernest Haller, A.S.C.
Film Editor	David Weisbart
Art Director	Anton de Grot
Montages by	James Leicester
Sound by	Oliver S. Garretson
Set Decorations by	George James Hopkins
Dialogue Director	Herschel Daugherty
Special Effects by	Willard van Enger, A.S.C.
Wardrobe by	Milo Anderson
Makeup Artist	Perc Westmore
Orchestral Arrangements by	Hugo Friedhofer
Musical Director	Leo F. Forbstein

Released: October 1945
Running time: 113 minutes

Cast

Mildred Pierce	Joan Crawford
Wally Fay	Jack Carson
Monte Beragon	Zachary Scott
Ida	Eve Arden
Veda Pierce	Ann Blyth
Bert Pierce	Bruce Bennett
Maggie Biederhof	Lee Patrick
Inspector Peterson	Moroni Olsen
Miriam	Veda Ann Borg
Kay Pierce	Jo Ann Marlowe
Mrs. Forrester	Barbara Brown
Mr. Williams	Charles Trowbridge
Ted Forrester	John Compton
Lottie	Butterfly McQueen
Mr. Jones	Chester Clute
Dr. Gale	Manart Kippen
Policeman on Pier	Garry Owen

Inventory

The following materials from the Warner library of the Wisconsin Center for Film and Theater Research were used by LaValley in preparing *Mildred Pierce* for the Wisconsin/Warner Bros. Screenplay Series.

Treatment, by Thames Williamson. January 21, 1944. 28 pages.

Temporary, by Catherine Turney. April 3 with revisions to May 12, 1944. Incomplete. 147 pages plus 10-page outline.

Comments, by Albert Maltz. May 25 to June 24, 1944. 62 pages.

Revised Temporary, by Turney. August 11, 1944. 194 pages.

Screenplay, by Margaret Gruen. September 16 to October 14, 1944. Incomplete. 149 pages plus 11-page outline.

Screenplay, by Ranald MacDougall. October 28 to December 2, 1944. Incomplete. 179 pages.

Screenplay, by William Faulkner. November 18 to December 2, 1944. 126 pages.

Screenplay, by Louise Pierson. November 27 to December 11, 1944. 119 pages.

Revised Final, by MacDougall. December 5, 1944, with revisions to February 24, 1945. 174 pages.

DESIGNED BY GARY GORE
COMPOSED BY THE NORTH CENTRAL PUBLISHING CO.
ST. PAUL, MINNESOTA
MANUFACTURED BY INTER-COLLEGIATE PRESS, INC.
SHAWNEE MISSION, KANSAS
TEXT AND DISPLAY LINES ARE SET IN PALATINO

Library of Congress Cataloging in Publication Data
MacDougall, Ranald.
Mildred Pierce.
(Wisconsin/Warner Bros. screenplay series)
"Screenplay by Ranald MacDougall,
from the novel by James M. Cain."
Includes bibliographical references.
I. LaValley, Albert J.
II. Cain, James Mallahan, 1892–1977. Mildred Pierce.
III. Wisconsin Center for Film and Theater Research
IV. Title. V. Series.
PN1997.M439   812'.54   80-5107
ISBN 0-299-08370-5
ISBN 0-299-08374-8 (pbk.)

WW

The Wisconsin/Warner Bros. Screenplay Series, a product of the Warner Brothers Film Library, will enable film scholars, students, researchers, and aficionados to gain insights into individual American films in ways never before possible.

The Warner library was acquired in 1957 by the United Artists Corporation, which in turn donated it to the Wisconsin Center for Film and Theater Research in 1969. The massive library, housed in the State Historical Society of Wisconsin, contains eight hundred sound feature films, fifteen hundred short subjects, and nineteen thousand still negatives, as well as the legal files, press books, and screenplays of virtually every Warner film produced from 1930 until 1950. This rich treasure trove has made the University of Wisconsin one of the major centers for film research, attracting scholars from around the world. This series of published screenplays represents a creative use of the Warner library, both a boon to scholars and a tribute to United Artists.

Most published film scripts are literal transcriptions of finished films. The Wisconsin/Warner screenplays are primary source documents—the final shooting versions including revisions made during production. As such, they will explicate the art of screenwriting as film transcriptions cannot. They will help the user to understand the arts of directing and acting, as well as the other arts involved in the film-making process, in comparing these screenplays with the final films. (Films of the Warner library are available at modest rates from the United Artists nontheatrical rental library, United Artists/16 mm.)

From the eight hundred feature films in the library, the general editor and the editorial committee of the series have chosen those that have received critical recognition for their excellence of directing, screenwriting, and acting, films that are distinctive examples of their genre, those that have particular historical relevance, and some that are adaptations of well-known novels and plays. The researcher, instructor, or student can, in the judicious selection of individual volumes for close examination, gain a heightened appreciation and broad understanding of the American film and its historical role during this critical period.